Mastering Matplotlib 2.x

Effective Data Visualization techniques with Python

Benjamin Walter Keller

BIRMINGHAM - MUMBAI

Mastering Matplotlib 2.x

Commissioning Editor: Pavan Ramchandani
Acquisition Editor: Dayne Castelino
Content Development Editor: Ronnel Mathew
Technical Editor: Sagar Sawant
Copy Editor: Safis Editing
Project Coordinator: Namrata Swetta
Proofreader: Safis Editing
Indexer: Tejal Daruwale Soni
Graphics: Jisha Chirayil
Production Coordinator: Jyoti Chauhan

First published: November 2018

Production reference: 1281118

Published by Packt Publishing Ltd.
Livery Place
35 Livery Street
Birmingham
B3 2PB, UK.

ISBN 978-1-78961-769-6

www.packtpub.com

`mapt.io`

Mapt is an online digital library that gives you full access to over 5,000 books and videos, as well as industry leading tools to help you plan your personal development and advance your career. For more information, please visit our website.

Why subscribe?

- Spend less time learning and more time coding with practical eBooks and Videos from over 4,000 industry professionals

- Improve your learning with Skill Plans built especially for you

- Get a free eBook or video every month

- Mapt is fully searchable

- Copy and paste, print, and bookmark content

Packt.com

Did you know that Packt offers eBook versions of every book published, with PDF and ePub files available? You can upgrade to the eBook version at `www.packt.com` and as a print book customer, you are entitled to a discount on the eBook copy. Get in touch with us at `customercare@packtpub.com` for more details.

At `www.packt.com`, you can also read a collection of free technical articles, sign up for a range of free newsletters, and receive exclusive discounts and offers on Packt books and eBooks.

Contributors

About the author

Benjamin Walter Keller is currently a PhD candidate at McMaster University and gained his BSc in physics with a minor in computer science from the University of Calgary in 2011. His current research involves numerical modeling of galaxy evolution over cosmological timescales. As an undergraduate at the U of C, he worked on stacking radio polarization to examine faint extragalactic sources. He also worked in the POSSUM Working Group 2 to determine the requirements for stacking applications for the Australian SKA Pathfinder (ASKAP) radio telescope. He is particularly interested in questions involving stellar feedback (supernovae, stellar winds, and so on) and its impact on galaxies and their surrounding intergalactic medium.

Packt is searching for authors like you

If you're interested in becoming an author for Packt, please visit `authors.packtpub.com` and apply today. We have worked with thousands of developers and tech professionals, just like you, to help them share their insight with the global tech community. You can make a general application, apply for a specific hot topic that we are recruiting an author for, or submit your own idea.

Table of Contents

Preface

Mastering Matplotlib covers use cases and unusual cases that require powerful tools. With easy-to-follow examples and the high-end components of Matplotlib, this book will enable you to develop advanced and interactive plots using Python scripting and Matplotlib.

Matplotlib is a multi-platform data visualization tool built upon the NumPy and SciPy frameworks. One of Matplotlib's most important features is its ability to work well with many operating systems and graphics backends.

In this book, you'll get hands-on with customizing your data plots with the help of Matplotlib. You'll start with customizing plots, making a handful of special-purpose plots, and building 3D plots. You'll explore non-trivial layouts, Pylab customization, and tile configuration. You'll be able to add text, put lines in plots, and also handle polygons, shapes, and annotations. Non-Cartesian and vector plots are exciting to construct, and you'll explore them further in this book. You'll delve into niche plots and visualize ordinal and tabular data.

In this book, you'll be exploring 3D plotting, one of the best features when it comes to 3D data visualization, along with Jupyter Notebook, widgets, and creating movies for enhanced data representation. Geospatial plotting will be also be explored. Finally, you'll learn how to create interactive plots with the help of Jupyter. By the end of this book, you'll be able to construct advanced plots with additional customization techniques and 3D plot types.

Who this book is for

This book is aimed at individuals who want to explore data visualization techniques. Basic knowledge of Matplotlib and Python is required.

What this book covers

Chapter 1, *Heavy Customization*, covers customizing Pylab and also learn about working on non-trivial layouts and the different Matplotlib configuration files.

Chapter 2, *Drawing on Plots*, explains how to put lines in place and add text to your plots. We will also learn about playing with polygons, shapes, and versatile annotating.

Chapter 3, *Special Purpose Plots*, covers non-Cartesian plots and plotting vector fields. We will also learn about statistics with boxes and violins, and also visualize ordinal and tabular data.

Chapter 4, *3D and Geospatial*, explores plotting with 3D axes, looking at the various 3D plot types and the Basemap methods. We will also learn about plotting on map projections and adding geography.

Chapter 5, *Interactive Plotting*, looks at interactive plots in Jupyter Notebook and event handling with plot callbacks. We will also learn about GUI neutral widgets and how to make movies.

To get the most out of this book

The readers should have basic knowledge of Python.

Download the example code files

You can download the example code files for this book from your account at www.packt.com. If you purchased this book elsewhere, you can visit www.packt.com/support and register to have the files emailed directly to you.

You can download the code files by following these steps:

1. Log in or register at www.packt.com.
2. Select the **SUPPORT** tab.
3. Click on **Code Downloads & Errata**.
4. Enter the name of the book in the **Search** box and follow the onscreen instructions.

Once the file is downloaded, please make sure that you unzip or extract the folder using the latest version of:

- WinRAR/7-Zip for Windows
- Zipeg/iZip/UnRarX for Mac
- 7-Zip/PeaZip for Linux

The code bundle for the book is also hosted on GitHub at https://github.com/PacktPublishing/Mastering-Matplotlib-2.x. In case there's an update to the code, it will be updated on the existing GitHub repository.

We also have other code bundles from our rich catalog of books and videos available at `https://github.com/PacktPublishing/`. Check them out!

Download the color images

We also provide a PDF file that has color images of the screenshots/diagrams used in this book. You can download it here: `http://www.packtpub.com/sites/default/files/downloads/9781789617696_ColorImages.pdf`.

Conventions used

There are a number of text conventions used throughout this book.

`CodeInText`: Indicates code words in text, database table names, folder names, filenames, file extensions, pathnames, dummy URLs, user input, and Twitter handles. Here is an example: "The easiest way to do this is to remove the `plot` keyword and call `semilogy`."

A block of code is set as follows:

```
import numpy as np
import matplotlib as mpl
import matplotlib.pyplot as plt
%matplotlib inline
```

Any command-line input or output is written as follows:

```
$ mkdir css
$ cd css
```

Bold: Indicates a new term, an important word, or words that you see onscreen. For example, words in menus or dialog boxes appear in the text like this. Here is an example: "Select **System info** from the **Administration** panel."

Warnings or important notes appear like this.

Tips and tricks appear like this.

Get in touch

Feedback from our readers is always welcome.

General feedback: If you have questions about any aspect of this book, mention the book title in the subject of your message and email us at customercare@packtpub.com.

Errata: Although we have taken every care to ensure the accuracy of our content, mistakes do happen. If you have found a mistake in this book, we would be grateful if you would report this to us. Please visit www.packt.com/submit-errata, selecting your book, clicking on the Errata Submission Form link, and entering the details.

Piracy: If you come across any illegal copies of our works in any form on the Internet, we would be grateful if you would provide us with the location address or website name. Please contact us at copyright@packt.com with a link to the material.

If you are interested in becoming an author: If there is a topic that you have expertise in and you are interested in either writing or contributing to a book, please visit authors.packtpub.com.

Reviews

Please leave a review. Once you have read and used this book, why not leave a review on the site that you purchased it from? Potential readers can then see and use your unbiased opinion to make purchase decisions, we at Packt can understand what you think about our products, and our authors can see your feedback on their book. Thank you!

For more information about Packt, please visit packt.com.

Heavy Customization

1

This book will teach us about advanced Matplotlib plots. It will enable you to go from data to plot to insight, in order to take raw numbers, raw information, and turn them into a visualization, which will allow us to build within our mind the actual bit of insight on how the data behaves. This will also focus on the advanced tools to derive more subtle insights from your data.

In this chapter, we will be focusing on the advanced tools of plotting so that you can really derive more subtle insights from your data. The prerequisites for this course give us a basic understanding of Python and the ability to use NumPy to work with array data.

We will learn about the following topics:

- Using style sheets to customize our plot's appearance
- Working with Matplotlib colors
- Building multi-panel plots with complex layouts
- How to configure Matplotlib to use our preferences whenever we start up a new Matplotlib session

Customizing PyLab using style

We will start by importing numpy, matplotlib, and pyplot, as follows:

```
import numpy as np
import matplotlib as mpl
import matplotlib.pyplot as plt
```

We will also import matplotlib and also import a couple of extra lines to make our plots show up in a proper format:

```
%matplotlib inline
# Set up figure size and DPI for screen demo
plt.rcParams['figure.figsize'] = (6,4)
```

```
plt.rcParams['figure.dpi'] = 150

from scipy.ndimage.filters import gaussian_filter
plt.subplot(221)
plt.text(0.5, 0.5, 'hello')
plt.plot(np.arange(0,1,0.01), np.power(np.arange(0,1,0.01), 3))
plt.ylabel('Axis Label')
plt.subplot(222)
plt.scatter(np.random.normal(size=10), np.random.normal(size=10),
c=np.random.normal(size=10))
plt.subplot(223)
plt.hist(np.random.normal(size=1000));
plt.hist(np.random.normal(1, size=1000));
plt.hist(np.random.normal(2, size=500));
plt.ylabel('Axis Label')
plt.xlabel('Axis Label')
plt.subplot(224)
plt.imshow(gaussian_filter(np.random.normal(size=(200,300)), sigma=10))
plt.xlabel('Axis Label')
```

We will begin with the preceding big block of code and will make an array—a little grid of four plots showing four basic plot types which includes a line plot (top left), a scatter plot (top right), a histogram (bottom left), and an image plot (bottom right), along with the respective axis labels:

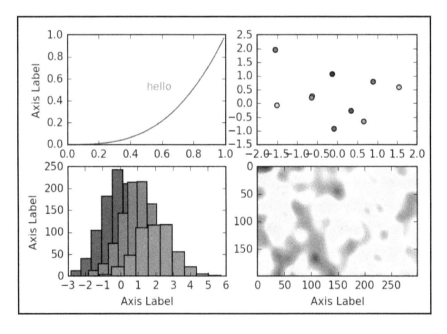

By default, Matplotlib will choose some fairly sensible choices for things like fonts, colors, and the other appearance attributes of these plots. These defaults aren't the only choices for appearance attributes that Matplotlib provides.

How to use styles to change the appearance of our plots

By using the style module within `pyplot`, you can see that when we call the function `available`, we actually get a list containing a number of different styles. Let's assume that each of these different styles acts to change the attributes and the appearance of the plots:

```
In [4]:   # What styles are available?
          plt.style.available

Out[4]:   ['bmh',
           'classic',
           'dark_background',
           'fivethirtyeight',
           'ggplot',
           'grayscale',
           'seaborn-bright',
           'seaborn-colorblind',
           'seaborn-dark-palette',
           'seaborn-dark',
           'seaborn-darkgrid',
           'seaborn-deep',
           'seaborn-muted',
           'seaborn-notebook',
           'seaborn-paper',
           'seaborn-pastel',
           'seaborn-poster',
           'seaborn-talk',
           'seaborn-ticks',
           'seaborn-white',
           'seaborn-whitegrid',
           'seaborn',
           '_classic_test']
```

So, by using the `plot.style.use` method, we can load up any one of these default style sheets. Using the `ggplot` (as shown in the preceding output) will actually mimic the appearance of the `ggplot` library, as you can see in the following code:

```
# Using styles
plt.style.use('dark_background')
from scipy.ndimage.filters import gaussian_filter
```

```
plt.subplot(221)
plt.plot(np.arange(0,1,0.01), np.power(np.arange(0,1,0.01), 3))
plt.ylabel('Axis Label')
plt.subplot(222)
plt.scatter(np.random.normal(size=10), np.random.normal(size=10),
c=np.random.normal(size=10))
plt.subplot(223)
plt.hist(np.random.normal(size=1000));
plt.hist(np.random.normal(1, size=1000));
plt.hist(np.random.normal(2, size=500));
plt.ylabel('Axis Label')
plt.xlabel('Axis Label')
plt.subplot(224)
plt.imshow(gaussian_filter(np.random.normal(size=(200,300)), sigma=10))
plt.xlabel('Axis Label')
```

After calling the `plt.style.use('ggplot')` method, we have the same kind of plots shown, but the axis objects and the appearance of these has been changed fairly significantly. There exists a white grid on a gray background, the fonts have changed as well as their colors, and the default color choices have changed as well.

Hence, we see that the histogram will have different colors, as shown in the following output:

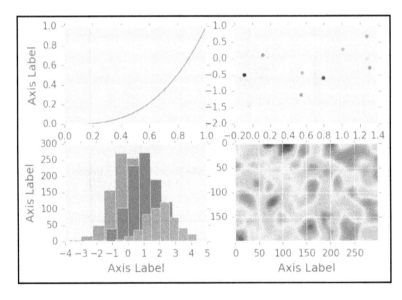

We can also change this to any other choice as well. If you're familiar with the Seaborn library, a Python library for doing more complicated analysis statistically, you can choose options that will mimic the Seaborn library:

```
# Using styles
plt.style.use('seaborn-talk')
from scipy.ndimage.filters import gaussian_filter
plt.subplot(221)
plt.plot(np.arange(0,1,0.01), np.power(np.arange(0,1,0.01), 3))
plt.ylabel('Axis Label')
plt.subplot(222)
plt.scatter(np.random.normal(size=10), np.random.normal(size=10),
c=np.random.normal(size=10))
plt.subplot(223)
plt.hist(np.random.normal(size=1000));
plt.hist(np.random.normal(1, size=1000));
plt.hist(np.random.normal(2, size=500));
plt.ylabel('Axis Label')
plt.xlabel('Axis Label')
plt.subplot(224)
plt.imshow(gaussian_filter(np.random.normal(size=(200,300)), sigma=10))
plt.xlabel('Axis Label')
```

Different Matplotlib styles

In this section, we will be learning about various styles provided by Matplotlib such as temporary styles or creating your own custom styles. The following are a few examples of different styles:

```
# Temporary styles
plt.style.use('classic')
from scipy.ndimage.filters import gaussian_filter
plt.subplot(221)
plt.plot(np.arange(0,1,0.01), np.power(np.arange(0,1,0.01), 3))
plt.ylabel('Axis Label')
plt.subplot(222)
with plt.style.context('ggplot'):
 plt.scatter(np.random.normal(size=10), np.random.normal(size=10),
c=np.random.normal(size=10))
plt.subplot(223)
plt.hist(np.random.normal(size=1000));
plt.hist(np.random.normal(1, size=1000));
plt.hist(np.random.normal(2, size=500));
plt.ylabel('Axis Label')
plt.xlabel('Axis Label')
plt.subplot(224)
```

```
plt.imshow(gaussian_filter(np.random.normal(size=(200,300)), sigma=10))
plt.xlabel('Axis Label')
```

Using the dark background will give you an image that shows up nicely on a dark background, hence if you're building slides, you might want to use the dark background style sheet:

```
# Custom styles
plt.style.use('bigpoints')
from scipy.ndimage.filters import gaussian_filter
plt.subplot(221)
plt.plot(np.arange(0,1,0.01), np.power(np.arange(0,1,0.01), 3), 'ko')
plt.ylabel('Axis Label')
plt.subplot(222)
plt.scatter(np.random.normal(size=10), np.random.normal(size=10),
c=np.random.normal(size=10))
plt.subplot(223)
plt.hist(np.random.normal(size=1000));
plt.hist(np.random.normal(1, size=1000));
plt.hist(np.random.normal(2, size=500));
plt.ylabel('Axis Label')
plt.xlabel('Axis Label')
plt.subplot(224)
plt.imshow(gaussian_filter(np.random.normal(size=(200,300)), sigma=10))
plt.xlabel('Axis Label')
```

You will see the output, which shows the black background:

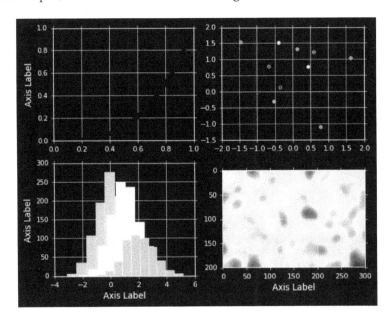

You can also choose style sheets temporarily. So, previously, we have chose a style sheet that affects all four plots. If, for example, I take my scatter plot and put it in a with `plt.style.context` block and choose a style sheet, let's say `ggplot`, you can see that we have actually overridden it, as shown here:

```
# Temporary styles
plt.style.use('classic')
from scipy.ndimage.filters import gaussian_filter
plt.subplot(221)
plt.plot(np.arange(0,1,0.01), np.power(np.arange(0,1,0.01), 3))
plt.ylabel('Axis Label')
plt.subplot(222)
with plt.style.context('ggplot'):
  plt.scatter(np.random.normal(size=10), np.random.normal(size=10),
c=np.random.normal(size=10))
plt.subplot(223)
plt.hist(np.random.normal(size=1000));
plt.hist(np.random.normal(1, size=1000));
plt.hist(np.random.normal(2, size=500));
plt.ylabel('Axis Label')
plt.xlabel('Axis Label')
plt.subplot(224)
plt.imshow(gaussian_filter(np.random.normal(size=(200,300)), sigma=10))
plt.xlabel('Axis Label')
```

From the preceding code, we can see there's a small difference, but the color map has changed:

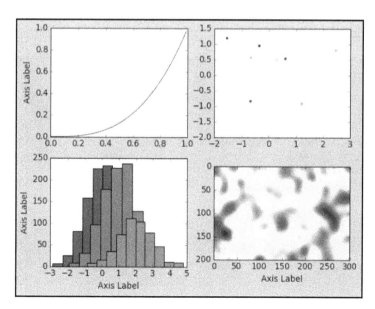

So, this one scatter plot has temporarily used a different set of choices for the appearance compared to the previous ones, so the other panels here are using the classic style sheet, whereas this is using `ggplot`, which changes the attributes of these points.

Creating your own styles

A question arises: can we actually make our own style sheet? The answer to that, of course, is **yes**. The first thing you need to know is where to put these style sheets.

So, when we run `mpl.get_configdir`, you can see we get a directory where the Matplotlib configuration options are stored and here we can actually place new style sheets:

```
# Where do we put out style sheets?
mpl.get_configdir()
```

We will thus generate our simple plot again by using a classic style sheet. Let's build a new style sheet; we will build something simple that will change just a single attribute. To build a new style sheet, we will follow these steps:

1. We will make a directory called `stylelib`—this will be where style files are actually stored, and these style sheets will live in this `stylelib` directory:

   ```
   $ ls
   $ mkdir stylelib
   $ cd stylelib
   ```

2. We will make one style sheet and name it `bigpoints.mplstyle`.

   `.mplstyle` is the file name extension for Matplotlib style sheets.

3. Insert the marker size and make it `20`:

   ```
   lines.markersize: 20
   ```

4. We will restart the kernel by clicking on the **Kernel** tab and then on **Restart** since we have created this new style sheet that only gets loaded in when Matplotlib is actually started up, as shown in the following screenshot:

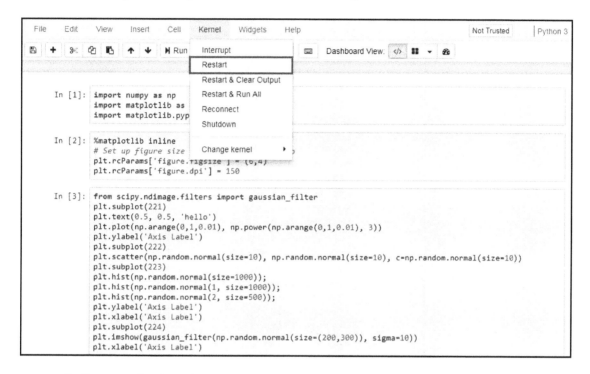

5. By going back to the Jupyter Notebook, we will reimport the following packages:

```
import numpy as np
import matplotlib as mpl
import matplotlib.pyplot as plt
%matplotlib inline
# Set up figure size and DPI for screen demo
plt.rcParams['figure.figsize'] = (6,4)
plt.rcParams['figure.dpi'] = 150
```

6. Next, we call `plt.style.available` and we see the addition to all of the big points, as shown in the following output:

```
In [4]:  # What styles are available?
         plt.style.available

Out[4]:  ['bmh',
          'classic',
          'dark_background',
          'fivethirtyeight',
          'ggplot',
          'grayscale',
          'seaborn-bright',
          'seaborn-colorblind',
          'seaborn-dark-palette',
          'seaborn-dark',
          'seaborn-darkgrid',
          'seaborn-deep',
          'seaborn-muted',
          'seaborn-notebook',
          'seaborn-paper',
          'seaborn-pastel',
          'seaborn-poster',
          'seaborn-talk',
          'seaborn-ticks',
          'seaborn-white',
          'seaborn-whitegrid',
          'seaborn',
          '_classic_test']
```

7. By running `plt.style.use('bigpoints')`, we can see it's changed the size of the points, as shown here:

```
# Custom styles
plt.style.use('bigpoints')
from scipy.ndimage.filters import gaussian_filter
plt.subplot(221)
plt.plot(np.arange(0,1,0.01), np.power(np.arange(0,1,0.01), 3))
plt.ylabel('Axis Label')
plt.subplot(222)
with plt.style.context('ggplot'):
    plt.scatter(np.random.normal(size=10),
np.random.normal(size=10), c=np.random.normal(size=10))
plt.subplot(223)
plt.hist(np.random.normal(size=1000));
```

```
plt.hist(np.random.normal(1, size=1000));
plt.hist(np.random.normal(2, size=500));
plt.ylabel('Axis Label')
plt.xlabel('Axis Label')
plt.subplot(224)
plt.imshow(gaussian_filter(np.random.normal(size=(200,300)),
sigma=10))
plt.xlabel('Axis Label')
```

We will get the following output:

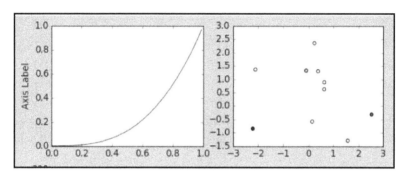

8. So, by typing `ko`, we get black dots. In the following image after the code snippet, you can see that those are quite big:

```
# Custom styles
plt.style.use('bigpoints')
from scipy.ndimage.filters import gaussian_filter
plt.subplot(221)
plt.plot(np.arange(0,1,0.01), np.power(np.arange(0,1,0.01), 3),
'ko')
plt.ylabel('Axis Label')
plt.subplot(222)
plt.scatter(np.random.normal(size=10), np.random.normal(size=10),
c=np.random.normal(size=10))
plt.subplot(223)
plt.hist(np.random.normal(size=1000));
plt.hist(np.random.normal(1, size=1000));
plt.hist(np.random.normal(2, size=500));
plt.ylabel('Axis Label')
plt.xlabel('Axis Label')
plt.subplot(224)
plt.imshow(gaussian_filter(np.random.normal(size=(200,300)),
sigma=10))
plt.xlabel('Axis Label')
```

From the preceding code, we get the following output:

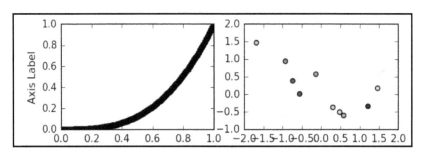

9. We will go back and edit this and insert 50 points (more than twice what was shown earlier):

    ```
    lines.markersize: 50
    ```

10. After reimporting `matplotlib`, run `plt.style.use('bigpoints')` using a new style sheet; we can see that the points are bigger than they were before.

Styles can also be composed using two sets of styles, so you can combine the attributes of two different style sheets to generate things that have different combinations, and the way to do that is actually to use a list for `plt.style.use`.

By typing `ggplot` and composing that with `dark_background`, all of the subsequent changes that the dark background provides overwrites the changes that `ggplot` provides:

```
# Composing styles
plt.style.use(['ggplot', 'dark background'])
from scipy.ndimage.filters import gaussian_filter
plt.subplot(221)
plt.plot(np.arange(0,1,0.01), np.power(np.arange(0,1,0.01), 3), 'ko')
plt.ylabel('Axis Label')
plt.subplot(222)
plt.scatter(np.random.normal(size=10), np.random.normal(size=10),
c=np.random.normal(size=10))
plt.subplot(223)
plt.hist(np.random.normal(size=1000));
plt.hist(np.random.normal(1, size=1000));
plt.hist(np.random.normal(2, size=500));
plt.ylabel('Axis Label')
plt.xlabel('Axis Label')
plt.subplot(224)
plt.imshow(gaussian_filter(np.random.normal(size=(200,300)), sigma=10))
plt.xlabel('Axis Label')
```

We will get the following output:

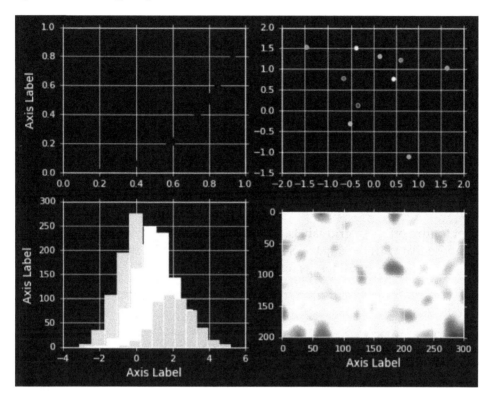

So, in other words, what we have here is a combination of ggplot modules and dark background changes, hence all of the things that ggplot changes, the dark background does not. All of the changes that both ggplot and the dark background change use the changes from the dark background, and all of the changes that ggplot does not make but the dark background does get applied.

It's kind of like an overwrite, wherein the dark background is applied after ggplot is applied. You can make custom style sheets and then compose them so that each style sheet can work together. So, for example, you can have a style sheet that will change line attributes that you can then compose with a style sheet that will change the axis or label attribute, and you can use that to modify the built-in default Matplotlib style sheets.

Taking an example, if you really loved the look of ggplot but you didn't quite like one little attribute of it, you could actually go in and change that, as follows:

```
# Composing styles
plt.style.use(['ggplot'])
```

```
from scipy.ndimage.filters import gaussian_filter
plt.subplot(221)
plt.plot(np.arange(0,1,0.01), np.power(np.arange(0,1,0.01), 3))
plt.ylabel('Axis Label')
plt.subplot(222)
plt.scatter(np.random.normal(size=10), np.random.normal(size=10),
c=np.random.normal(size=10))
plt.subplot(223)
plt.hist(np.random.normal(size=1000));
plt.hist(np.random.normal(1, size=1000));
plt.hist(np.random.normal(2, size=500));
plt.ylabel('Axis Label')
plt.xlabel('Axis Label')
plt.subplot(224)
plt.imshow(gaussian_filter(np.random.normal(size=(200,300)), sigma=10))
plt.xlabel('Axis Label')
```

If you want to turn off these grid labels, you can create a new style sheet, disable grid labels, compose that with the ggplot style sheet, and get a plot that looks exactly the same but without those white grid lines, as follows:

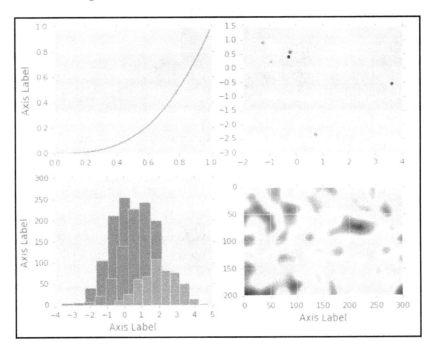

In the next section, we are going to take a deep dive into looking at colors within Matplotlib and how to configure and customize them.

Deep diving into color

When it comes to choosing color maps, we have a near infinite set of choices available to us, so it makes a lot of sense to think about the theory of why certain color maps are designed in the way they are.

A classic paper on the theory of *Choosing a Colour Sequence for Univariate Maps* was published by Colin Ware over 30 years ago. In this paper, Dr. Ware defines two different important things to think about when choosing a color map:

- How a color map conveys the metric value of individual points within the image
- How that color map conveys form—the shape of the different points interacting within each other

Questions to ask when choosing a color map

Different color maps can perform better or worse at conveying metrics, letting the viewer know the value of pixels on the screen, and conveying form—showing how those pixels relate to one another. Whether or not form or metrics or both are important for a given image is really key to deciding what kind of color map to use for that image.

The different questions that can be asked when choosing a color map are as follows:

- Do we need to think whether or not the shape, the value, or-again-both are important for that field?
- Are there critical values or transitions in the data?
- Are there ranges of numbers that really want to pop out to the viewer?
- What is the intuitive choice of colors for the dataset?

For most people, a dataset that conveys temperature should usually have hot red colors to denote high temperatures and cool blue colors to denote cold temperatures; to reverse that would violate the intuitive sense that the viewer has and set up an initial set of stressors in their mind that's going to make interpreting the image harder than it needs to be.

Taking an example, have a look at the color map here, showing population density in the United States:

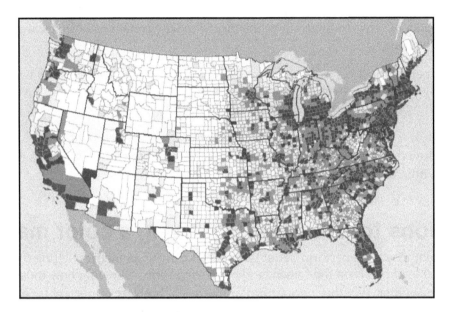

Using one kind of color map—one that's not perceptually uniform—washes out a lot of the high values. Simply changing it to another different kind of color map that has less high-valued whitish colors at the high end allows you to see more detail in the higher density, more populated eastern parts of the US.

To take a look at all of the color maps that Matplotlib provides, visit the website provided here: `http://matplotlib.org/examples/color/colormaps_reference.html`. This offers a little swatch of each different color map to give you an idea of what the color map can do in terms of the ranges.

Before we move ahead with the code, we will start by importing the following set of default packages, as shown here:

```
import numpy as np
import matplotlib as mpl
import matplotlib.pyplot as plt

%matplotlib inline
# Set up figure size and DPI for screen demo
plt.rcParams['figure.figsize'] = (6,4)
plt.rcParams['figure.dpi'] = 150
```

Using color maps

Now, we can choose a color map from Matplotlib's selection of color maps by passing the
`cmap='inferno'` color map:

```
from scipy.ndimage.filters import gaussian_filter
plt.imshow(gaussian_filter(np.random.normal(size=(200,300)), sigma=10))
```

The following displays the image using the inferno color map:

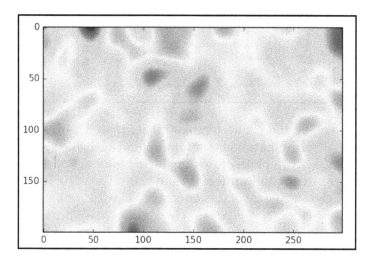

We can see the differences in the value between dark cool colors and white hot colors. The
perceptually uniform color maps are good at conveying both metric and form. There are
color maps that you might want to choose for different kinds of purposes.

For example, the seismic color map, which is one of the diverging color maps, is very good
for showing differences between the middle values of your plot. So, divergences towards
the highly positive or highly negative in most of the values near the median of the pixels
are hard to distinguish. What instead pops out to the viewer are the highly positive and
highly negative ranges, as shown in the following code and image:

```
from scipy.ndimage.filters import gaussian_filter
plt.imshow(gaussian_filter(np.random.normal(size=(200,300)), sigma=10),
cmap='seismic')
```

The following is the output of the preceding code:

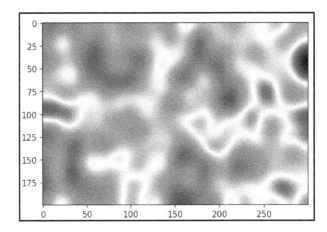

Another option is one of the miscellaneous color maps, `flag`. This is a really good example of a color map that maximizes the amount of information available in terms of the form that is the shape of the data, but completely loses any metric information. This color map actually cycles, so there are multiple different values corresponding to red, white, black, and blue. In a way, it gives you a set of contours much like the contour command does:

```
# Choose a new colormap
from scipy.ndimage.filters import gaussian_filter
plt.imshow(gaussian_filter(np.random.normal(size=(200,300)), sigma=10),
cmap='flag')
```

The following is the output of the preceding code:

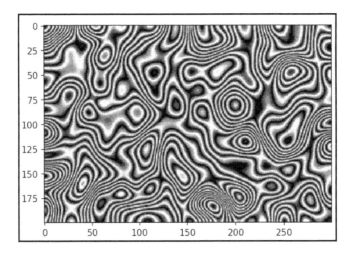

We can create our own color maps using Matplotlib's colors module. We can create a color map using the listed method from colors that will create a color map from a list of named colors available for our image. So, it will actually create something that looks a lot like a filled contour plot:

```
# Generate a custom discrete colormap w/ ListedColormap
from matplotlib import colors
from scipy.ndimage.filters import gaussian_filter
plt.imshow(gaussian_filter(np.random.normal(size=(200,300)), sigma=10),
cmap=colors.ListedColormap(['r', 'b', 'g']))
plt.colorbar()
```

Hence, from the preceding code, we get the output contour map showing that the colors are split into three separate pieces. The following plot shows a discrete color map, again, something that's very good for showing form but not particularly good for showing metrics unless we had to include a large range of colors that would split this up and make it more continuous:

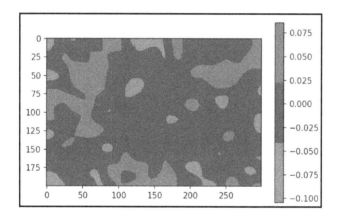

Now, this linear segmented color map requires a call structure, which is a basic `ListedColor`.

We will include the first argument as my_map as we are creating a new one, which also requires a dictionary as its second argument, called `cdict`:

```
# Generate a custom discrete colormap w/ LinearSegmentedColormap
cdict = dict(red=[(0, 0, 0.5), (0.5, 1, 0.5), (1, 1, 0.5)],
            green=[(0,0,1), (1, 0, 1)],
            blue=[(0, 0, 1), (1, 0, 1)])
plt.imshow(gaussian_filter(np.random.normal(size=(200,300)), sigma=10),
cmap=colors.LinearSegmentedColormap('my_map',cdict))
plt.colorbar()
```

In the preceding code, we can see that there are three keyword arguments: `red`, `green`, and `blue`. Each of these is itself a list and these lists have elements that are three-element tuples; these tuples can be seen for the initial and last elements for the colors red, green, and blue.

Each of the three numbers in this tuple corresponds to the start value of that segment, the amount of that color we get in that value of the segment, and the alpha or transparency of that value in the segment. In the preceding plot, the color red becomes fully saturated at the end of our color map. The color red contains an extra element in the middle when we reach full saturation, as shown in the following colored map:

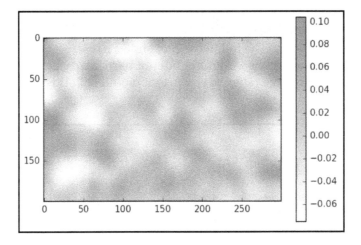

Adding a bit of opacity that allows between 0 and 0.5, as shown in the preceding code snippet, we get the following output:

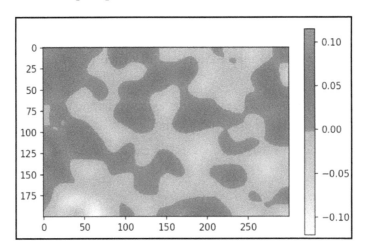

The previous output shows a linear segmented color map which is a way to create any kind of complex sophisticated color map.

Let's look at another example, where colors are important in Matplotlib. We have seen already that the Matplotlib backend will automatically cycle through colors, so you can see in the next output that there are different waveforms:

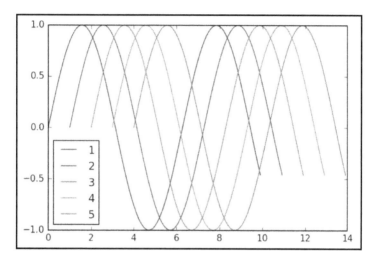

To reset and interchange the colors, the axis object we learned has a set_prop_cycle argument. That cycler decides what the next color should be, so if we set the prop cycle to None after every second set of plot commands, we can see that the cycle changes the color and loops again, as follows:

```
# Color cycler: reset with Axes set_prop_cycle(None) method
nums = np.arange(0,10,0.1)
plt.plot(nums, np.sin(nums), label='1')
plt.plot(1+nums, np.sin(nums), label='2')
plt.gca().set_prop_cycle(None)
plt.plot(2+nums, np.sin(nums), label='3')
plt.plot(3+nums, np.sin(nums), label='4')
plt.gca().set_prop_cycle(None)
plt.plot(4+nums, np.sin(nums), label='5')
plt.legend(loc='best')
```

We will get the following output:

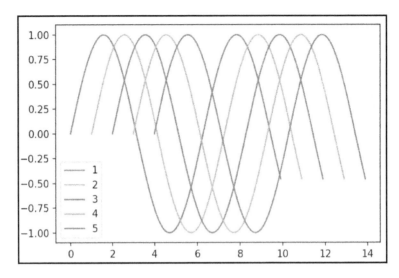

We reset and go back to the beginning, but not only can we set this to None to reset our cycler, we can use the cycler module that Matplotlib provides. It's actually its own module, so we will import the cycler from itself and not from Matplotlib. By setting the prop cycle to the new color cycler, we can actually define our own cycler.

We have created a cycler that goes from red to blue. We will include another one here, which is cyan, hence we should go from red to cyan to blue and then loop over those again, as seen in the following code:

```
# Color cycler: custom with cycler
from cycler import cycler
color_cyc = cycler('color', ['red', 'cyan', 'blue'])
plt.gca().set_prop_cycle(color_cyc)
nums = np.arange(0,10,0.1)
plt.plot(nums, np.sin(nums), label='1')
plt.plot(1+nums, np.sin(nums), label='2')
plt.plot(2+nums, np.sin(nums), label='3')
plt.plot(3+nums, np.sin(nums), label='4')
plt.plot(4+nums, np.sin(nums), label='5')
plt.legend(loc='best')
```

Hence, here, we get the following output:

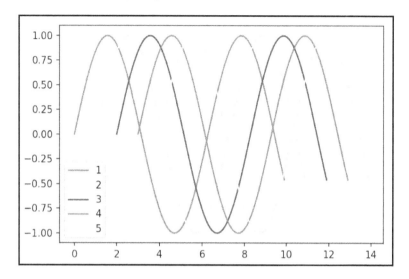

This is a way of setting up your own set of color cycles, so, for example, if there are lines that have relationships to each other—so say you want to go throughout the red-orange-yellow-green-blue-indigo-violet spectrum with regards to your lines rather than the built-in cycle that Matplotlib provides—you can use this cycler to do it.

Working on non-trivial layouts

We will begin by looking at a subplot with one set of rows and three columns, as shown here:

```
# Standard Subplot
plt.subplot(131)
plt.subplot(132)
plt.subplot(133)
```

The following is the output of the preceding input:

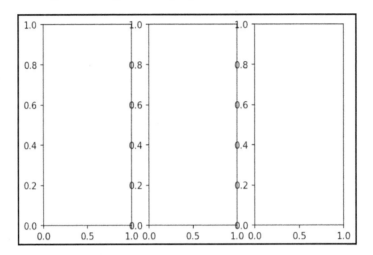

Now, by default, it will provide three plots side by side of equal size, but if we want them on top of each other instead, we will choose three rows and one column:

```
# Standard Subplot
plt.subplot(311)
plt.subplot(312)
plt.subplot(313)
```

We will get the following output:

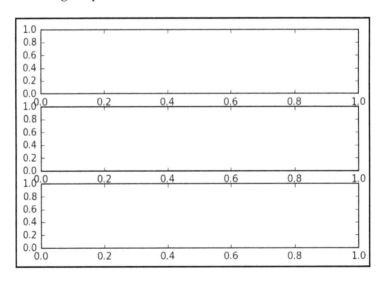

But what if these plots aren't necessarily supposed to show three identical ranges? In that case, we have the `subplot2grid` method:

```
# subplot2grid
plt.subplot2grid((2,2), (0,0))
plt.subplot2grid((2,2), (1,0))
plt.subplot2grid((2,2), (0,1))
```

We will begin by making the same vertical plot as shown previously. Now, specify one row and three columns and in the second tuple, select the rows, because there's only one and three columns. Next, we will see that there's a grid with two rows and three columns. We will place everything in the first column within the first row and simply specify a column:

```
# subplot2grid
plt.subplot2grid((2,3), (0,0))
plt.subplot2grid((2,3), (0,1))
plt.subplot2grid((2,3), (0,2))
```

The output will be as follows:

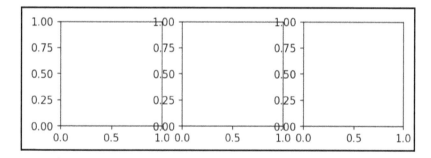

Now, to get this in a 2 x 3 grid, we need to have two plots underneath a third one; well in that case, what we want is a 2 x 2 grid, so one plot is going to be twice as wide and then two plots beneath, as shown here:

```
# Adjusting GridSpec attributes: w/h space
gs = mpl.gridspec.GridSpec(2,2)
plt.subplot(gs[0,0])
plt.subplot(gs[1,0])
plt.subplot(gs[1,1])
```

We will get the following output:

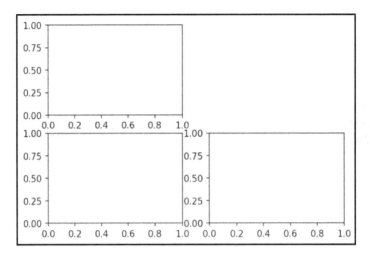

We have the positions right, but this has not actually made the plots bigger. To do that, we will have to pass an argument to the first one, `plt.subplot2grid`, called `colspan=2`, and using `colspan`, we say that this plot should span as shown in the following code:

```
# subplot2grid
plt.subplot2grid((2,2), (0,0), colspan=2)
plt.subplot2grid((2,2), (1,0))
plt.subplot2grid((2,2), (0,1))
```

We will get the following output::

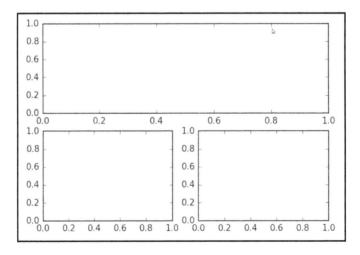

There is also another option as well for doing similar things, but in the vertical direction with row span. Therefore, we can perform the following action:

```
# subplot2grid
plt.subplot2grid((2,2), (0,0))
plt.subplot2grid((2,2), (1,0))
plt.subplot2grid((2,2), (0,1), rowspan=2)
```

From the preceding code, we will get the following output:

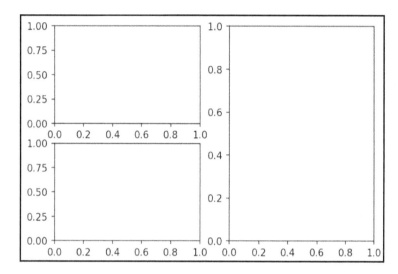

We can do the same thing using a `GridSpec` object and in fact we can customize this a little more explicitly. After creating a `GridSpec` object, iterate it through the indices of that `GridSpec` to say where it will get placed. These indices are just like any two-dimensional NumPy array. So, for example, we can perform the following:

```
# Explicit GridSpec
gs = mpl.gridspec.GridSpec(2,2)
plt.subplot(gs[0,0])
plt.subplot(gs[0,1])
```

The following is the output of the preceding code:

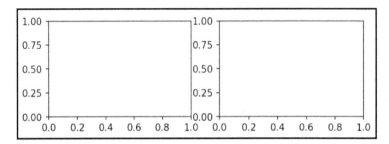

By including a diagonal pair of plots, we get the following:

```
# Explicit GridSpec
gs = mpl.gridspec.GridSpec(2,2)
plt.subplot(gs[0,0])
plt.subplot(gs[1,1])
```

We will get the following output:

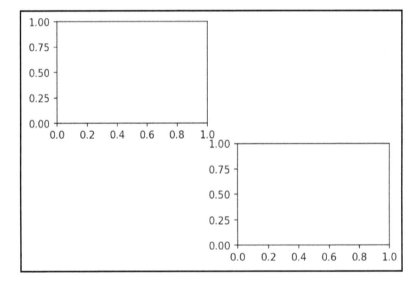

We can also make those plots span things using the range syntax that NumPy provides for us:

```
# Explicit GridSpec
gs = mpl.gridspec.GridSpec(2,2)
plt.subplot(gs[0,:])
plt.subplot(gs[1,1])
```

The preceding code gives the following output:

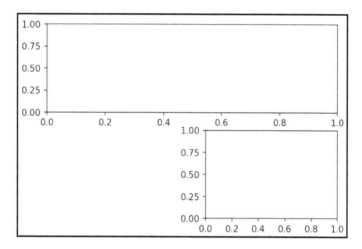

If, for example, we made this have three columns, we would get the following:

```
# Explicit GridSpec
gs = mpl.gridspec.GridSpec(2,3)
plt.subplot(gs[0,:])
plt.subplot(gs[1,1])
```

We will get the following output:

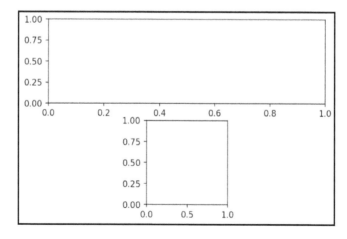

This shows that we can really dive into providing whatever kind of grid-like layout we want with plots of different sizes and shapes. You can also customize the amount of space between these plots. For example, look at the following grid:

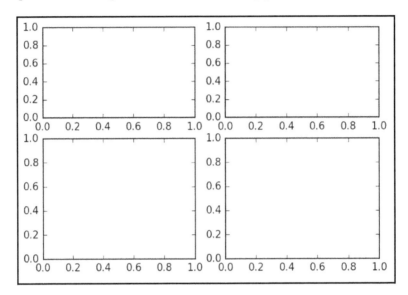

We can adjust the amount of space between the grids using `wspace` for space between the plots:

```
# Adjusting GridSpec attributes: w/h space
gs = mpl.gridspec.GridSpec(2,2, wspace=0.5)
plt.subplot(gs[0,0])
plt.subplot(gs[0,1])
plt.subplot(gs[1,0])
plt.subplot(gs[1,1])
```

The preceding code gives the following output:

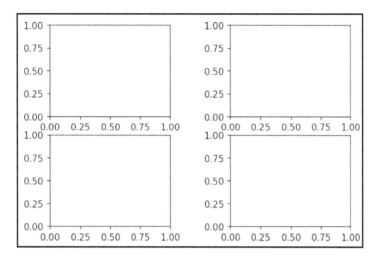

We can also adjust the amount of space between the grids using `hspace` for space between the plots:

```
# Adjusting GridSpec attributes: w/h space
gs = mpl.gridspec.GridSpec(2,2, hspace=0.5)
plt.subplot(gs[0,0])
plt.subplot(gs[0,1])
plt.subplot(gs[1,0])
plt.subplot(gs[1,1])
```

The ratios of the sizes can also be changed between the plots. So, say, for example, that we want our top row to be very tall and thin; we can specify a width and height ratio. If we pass `width_ratios`, we can decide how big each of these columns will appear relative to one another in terms of their width:

```
# Adjusting GridSpec attributes: width/height ratio
gs = mpl.gridspec.GridSpec(2,2, width_ratio=(1,2))
plt.subplot(gs[0,0])
plt.subplot(gs[0,1])
plt.subplot(gs[1,0])
plt.subplot(gs[1,1])
```

It sets the width of the second column to be twice the width of the first column:

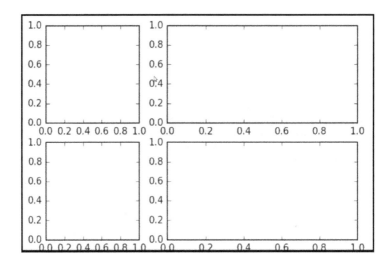

When changing this to (2, 2), they will be equal, so it will literally just take a ratio of these numbers; you can pass whatever pair of ratios you want:

```
# Adjusting GridSpec attributes: width/height ratio
gs = mpl.gridspec.GridSpec(2,2, width_ratio=(2,2))
plt.subplot(gs[0,0])
plt.subplot(gs[0,1])
plt.subplot(gs[1,0])
plt.subplot(gs[1,1])
```

We will get the following output:

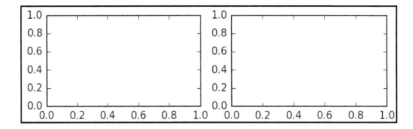

By changing the heights, we get the second set of plots—twice the height of the first one, as shown here:

```
# Adjusting GridSpec attributes: width/height ratio
gs = mpl.gridspec.GridSpec(2,2, height_ratio=(1,2))
plt.subplot(gs[0,0])
plt.subplot(gs[0,1])
plt.subplot(gs[1,0])
plt.subplot(gs[1,1])
```

We will see the following output:

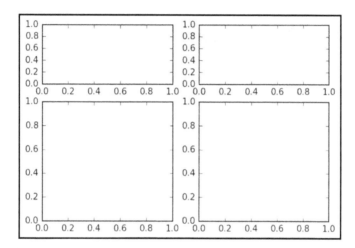

These cannot only be integers—they can be floating-point numbers as well, as shown here:

```
# Adjusting GridSpec attributes: width/height ratio
gs = mpl.gridspec.GridSpec(2,2, height_ratios=(1.5,2))
plt.subplot(gs[0,0])
plt.subplot(gs[0,1])
plt.subplot(gs[1,0])
plt.subplot(gs[1,1])
```

By executing the preceding code, we will get the following output:

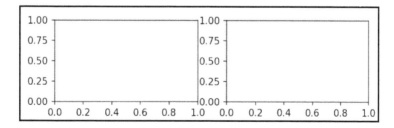

Hence, this is a quick and convenient way of setting up multi-panel plots that put the focus on the kinds of plots that we want to dominate. So, if you have a situation where, for example, you have a complex dataset where one piece of that visualization is the most important one but you have many supplemental plots that you want to show alongside it, using the subplot two grid and the grid spec object can be a nice way of building up those layouts.

The Matplotlib configuration files

In this section, we will look at the `matplotlib` configuration file, `matplotlibrc`, which contains all of the default configuration settings for how Matplotlib works on your system.

Matplotlibrc – where does it live?

`matplotlibrc` is multiple different configuration files; it's a hierarchy of configuration files that allows you to configure Matplotlib to behave differently for different users or different projects depending on what you need. By default, the hierarchy of which `matplotlibrc` config file overrides others begins with the one in the current directory, which oftentimes does not exist but ultimately will be the one that overrides all others.

The next one is within the `matplotlibrc` environment variable in that directory.

The third is within the config home, if you're running a Linux or BSD-based operating system with a directory called Matplotlib and a file called `matplotlibrc`.

Finally, with the Matplotlib installation pending on what system you're on, that installation living in some install directory will have a directory called **Matplotlib data**. A Matplotlib RC file that comes with Matplotlib installation is actually a fairly rich template that includes a wide variety of comments and example code which we will be discussing.

We will take a copy of the example file and put it in the `.config/matplotlib` file.

After opening the configuration file, we can see that it is quite big—in fact, it's 510 lines by default with the current version of Matplotlib, as shown here:

```
 1   ### MATPLOTLIBRC FORMAT
 2
 3   # This is a sample matplotlib configuration file - you can find a copy
 4   # of it on your system in
 5   # site-packages/matplotlib/mpl-data/matplotlibrc.  If you edit it
 6   # there, please note that it will be overwritten in your next install.
 7   # If you want to keep a permanent local copy that will not be
 8   # overwritten, place it in the following location:
 9   # unix/linux:
10   #      $HOME/.config/matplotlib/matplotlibrc or
11   #      $XDG_CONFIG_HOME/matplotlib/matplotlibrc (if $XDG_CONFIG_HOME is set)
12   # other platforms:
13   #      $HOME/.matplotlib/matplotlibrc
14   #
15   # See http://matplotlib.org/users/customizing.html#the-matplotlibrc-file for
16   # more details on the paths which are checked for the configuration file.
17   #
18   # This file is best viewed in a editor which supports python mode
19   # syntax highlighting. Blank lines, or lines starting with a comment
20   # symbol, are ignored, as are trailing comments.  Other lines must
21   # have the format
22   #    key : val # optional comment
23   #
24   # Colors: for the color values below, you can either use - a
25   # matplotlib color string, such as r, k, or b - an rgb tuple, such as
```

It also has a number of different options for configuring things such as fonts and appearance, as shown here:

```
133   # The font.stretch property has 11 values: ultra-condensed,
134   # extra-condensed, condensed, semi-condensed, normal, semi-expanded,
135   # expanded, extra-expanded, ultra-expanded, wider, and narrower.  This
136   # property is not currently implemented.
137   #
138   # The font.size property is the default font size for text, given in pts.
139   # 12pt is the standard value.
140   #
141   #font.family         : sans-serif
142   #font.style          : normal
143   #font.variant        : normal
144   #font.weight         : medium
145   #font.stretch        : normal
```

There are also options such as the Latex behavior:

```
165  ### LaTeX customizations. See http://wiki.scipy.org/Cookbook/Matplotlib/UsingTex
166  #text.usetex        : False  # use latex for all text handling. The following fonts
167                              # are supported through the usual rc parameter settings:
168                              # new century schoolbook, bookman, times, palatino,
169                              # zapf chancery, charter, serif, sans-serif, helvetica,
170                              # avant garde, courier, monospace, computer modern roman,
171                              # computer modern sans serif, computer modern typewriter
172                              # If another font is desired which can loaded using the
173                              # LaTeX \usepackage command, please inquire at the
174                              # matplotlib mailing list
175  #text.latex.unicode : False # use "ucs" and "inputenc" LaTeX packages for handling
176                          # unicode strings.
177  #text.latex.preamble :   # IMPROPER USE OF THIS FEATURE WILL LEAD TO LATEX FAILURES
```

There are also options for the behavior of different backends, and we can configure the options that do not necessarily get covered by style sheets that would just be things like appearance, as follows:

```
419  # tk backend params
420  #tk.window_focus    : False     # Maintain shell focus for TkAgg
421
422  # ps backend params
423  #ps.papersize        : letter   # auto, letter, legal, ledger, A0-A10, B0-B10
424  #ps.useafm           : False    # use of afm fonts, results in small files
425  #ps.usedistiller     : False    # can be: None, ghostscript or xpdf
426                                  # Experimental: may produce smaller files.
427                                  # xpdf intended for production of publication quality files,
428                                  # but requires ghostscript, xpdf and ps2eps
429  #ps.distiller.res   : 6000      # dpi
430  #ps.fonttype        : 3         # Output Type 3 (Type3) or Type 42 (TrueType)
431
432  # pdf backend params
433  #pdf.compression    : 6 # integer from 0 to 9
434                          # 0 disables compression (good for debugging)
435  #pdf.fonttype       : 3          # Output Type 3 (Type3) or Type 42 (TrueType)
436
437  # svg backend params
438  #svg.image_inline : True        # write raster image data directly into the svg file
```

The following screenshot shows the SVG writer:

```
437  # svg backend params
438  #svg.image_inline : True        # write raster image data directly into the svg file
439  #svg.image_noscale : False      # suppress scaling of raster data embedded in SVG
440  #svg.fonttype : 'path'          # How to handle SVG fonts:
441  #    'none': Assume fonts are installed on the machine where the SVG will be viewed.
442  #    'path': Embed characters as paths -- supported by most SVG renderers
443  #    'svgfont': Embed characters as SVG fonts -- supported only by Chrome,
444  #             Opera and Safari
```

Also, taking an example on what the default backend is, by default, we will set the backend to be `TkAgg`. We can, of course, change this depending on the system:

```
# The default backend; one of GTK GTKAgg GTKCairo GTK3Agg GTK3Cairo
# CocoaAgg MacOSX Qt4Agg Qt5Agg TkAgg WX WXAgg Agg Cairo GDK PS PDF SVG
# Template.
# You can also deploy your own backend outside of matplotlib by
# referring to the module name (which must be in the PYTHONPATH) as
# 'module://my_backend'.
backend      : TkAgg
```

For example, we can change the color of text, as shown here:

```
# text.color : black
```

After uncommenting `text.color` (since this ultimately is the highest `matplotlibrc` in that hierarchy, overwriting versions of the `.config` file), there isn't a custom version in the directory with the Jupyter Notebooks. We will restart the kernel like we did earlier in this chapter:

Reimporting NumPy and Matplotlib, we can see here that after adding some text, `hello`, and inserting `0.5`, we can see the colored text automatically without having to specify any other configuration options that you apply would get automatically applied without having to go in and change things by hand:

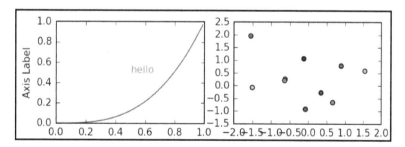

It's recommended to see all of the different options that Matplotlib provides. Go and take a look at that default template file:

```
 1   ### MATPLOTLIBRC FORMAT
 2
 3   # This is a sample matplotlib configuration file - you can find a copy
 4   # of it on your system in
 5   # site-packages/matplotlib/mpl-data/matplotlibrc.  If you edit it
 6   # there, please note that it will be overwritten in your next install.
 7   # If you want to keep a permanent local copy that will not be
 8   # overwritten, place it in the following location:
 9   # unix/linux:
10   #       $HOME/.config/matplotlib/matplotlibrc or
11   #       $XDG_CONFIG_HOME/matplotlib/matplotlibrc (if $XDG_CONFIG_HOME is set)
12   # other platforms:
13   #       $HOME/.matplotlib/matplotlibrc
```

Also, take a look at this documentation here: `http://matplotlib.org/users/customizing.html#the-matplotlibrc-file`. There is a little bit of extra text about the Matplotlib RC file. The template itself contains enough documentation. Understand this config file and look at all of the various options that are available to you.

So, if you want to configure your Matplotlib to behave in a more sensible way for your projects, it is recommended that you make a copy of this and start hacking away at it to tweak Matplotlib to do exactly what it is that you want it to.

Summary

In this chapter, we have learned about how to use style sheets to customize plot appearances, how to work with the color system within Matplotlib, how to tweak multi-panel plots to give more complex and appealing layouts for different kinds of plotting applications, and finally how to configure our Matplotlib installation.

In the next chapter, we will learn how to draw on plots to add annotations and highlights to really make the important features of a visualization pop out to the viewer.

2
Drawing on Plots

Till now, we have studied how to use style sheets to customize plot appearances, and how to tweak multi-panel plots to give more complex and appealing layouts for different kinds of plotting applications.

Matplotlib allows you to make plots that really show your own individual style. We will learn how to draw on plots to provide the viewer with visual guides that point them toward the important features of data. We will discuss adding horizontal and vertical lines, along with tweaking a background grid.

Versatile annotating adds arrows and some text to these arrows to the plots in order to customize the appearance of these annotations.

In this chapter, we will look at the following topics:

- How to put lines in place
- How to add text on plots
- How to play with polygons and shapes
- How to add different kinds of annotations

Putting lines in place

This section describes adding horizontal and vertical lines along with adding and tweaking a background grid.

Adding horizontal and vertical lines

We will begin by importing our required libraries, as shown:

```
import numpy as np
import matplotlib as mpl
import matplotlib.pyplot as plt
%matplotlib inline
# Set up figure size and DPI for screen demo
plt.rcParams['figure.figsize'] = (6,4)
plt.rcParams['figure.dpi'] = 150
```

1. We will create the simple sine plot that we saw in Chapter 1, *Heavy Customization*, as follows:

   ```
   # Adding a horizontal and vertical line
   nums = np.arange(0,10,0.1)
   plt.plot(nums, np.sin(nums))
   ```

   We will get the following output:

   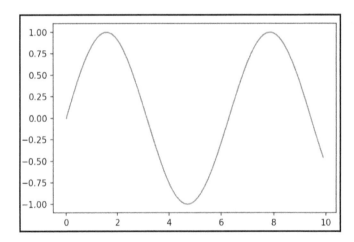

2. Now, to add an annotation, say, a line that splits the region between stuff above and below 0.5, add a horizontal line using axhline(0.5), as shown here. ax stands for the *x* axis and gives a value in the *y* co-ordinate for the horizontal line:

   ```
   # Adding a horizontal and vertical line
   nums = np.arange(0,10,0.1)
   plt.plot(nums, np.sin(nums))
   plt.axhline(0.5)
   ```

We will get the following output:

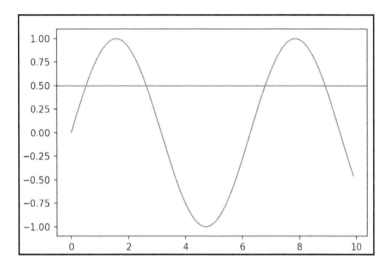

3. To color this horizontal line red, insert the following code:

```
# Adding a horizontal and vertical line
nums = np.arange(0,10,0.1)
plt.plot(nums, np.sin(nums))
plt.axhline(0.5, color='r')
```

We will get the following output:

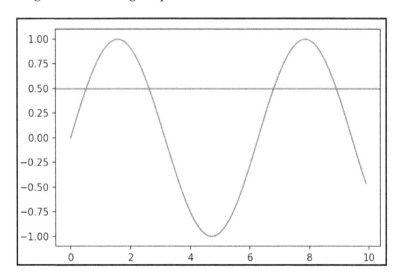

4. To add a vertical line right at the first maximum, input `pi/2` and color this red, along with a dashed line:

```
# Adding a horizontal and vertical line
nums = np.arange(0,10,0.1)
plt.plot(nums, np.sin(nums))
plt.axhline(0.5, color='r')
plt.axvline(np.pi/2., color='r', linestyle='--')
```

Here we can see `axv` for the vertical line instead of `axhline`:

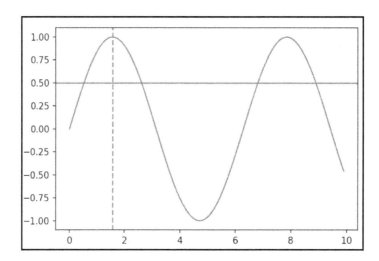

Adding spans that cover whole regions

To color the whole region, say between 0.5 and -0.5, insert the horizontal span as follows:

```
# Adding a horizontal and vertical span
nums = np.arange(0,10,0.1)
plt.plot(nums, np.sin(nums))
plt.axhspan(-0.5,0.5)
```

We get the output here as follows:

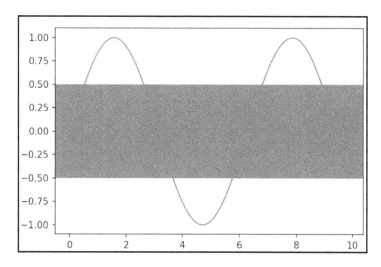

But the shaded region blocks out a lot of our data. Hence, we will make this black and give it an `alpha` of `0.5`, as follows:

```
# Adding a horizontal and vertical span
nums = np.arange(0,10,0.1)
plt.plot(nums, np.sin(nums))
plt.axhspan(-0.5,0.5, alpha=0.5)
```

We will get the following output:

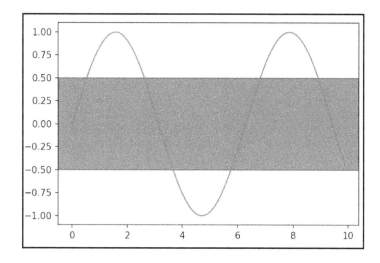

Performing the same thing for a vertical span will give you a region between -0.5 and 0.5. Just like any of the other plotting commands that involve areas, we can give this hatches, change the color of it, and add any of the appearance attributes as well, as shown in the following code:

```
# Adding a horizontal and vertical span
nums = np.arange(0,10,0.1)
plt.plot(nums, np.sin(nums))
plt.axvspan(-0.5,0.5, color='k', alpha=0.5)
```

The output can be seen as follows:

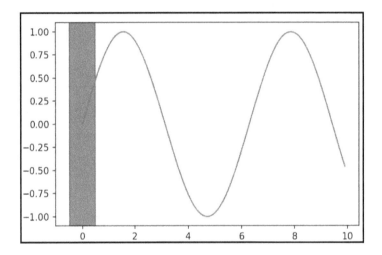

We can also set how far the vertical line goes across the axis. By default, the vertical line covers up the entire axis, as follows:

```
# Adding a horizontal and vertical span
nums = np.arange(0,10,0.1)
plt.plot(nums, np.sin(nums))
plt.axhspan(-0.5,0.5, alpha=0.5)
```

We will get the following output:

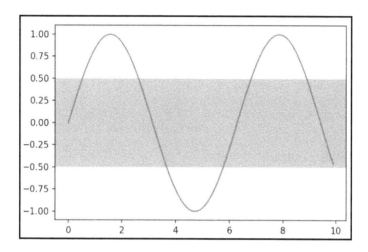

Now, if we pass a third keyword argument, xmin, we can give a minimum value, and xmax as the maximum value. Importantly, these are in the coordinates of the axis, so they go from 0 to 1, as shown in the following code:

```
# Span Axis coverage (min/max)
nums = np.arange(0,10,0.1)
plt.plot(nums, np.sin(nums))
plt.axhspan(-0.5,0.5, xmin=0, xmax=1, alpha=0.5)
```

From the preceding code, we get the following output::

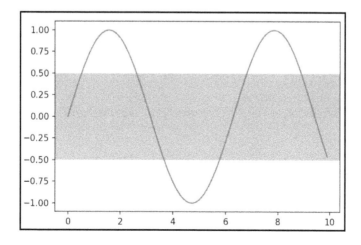

Note that in the data dimensions, the coordinates go from 0 to 10. But as usual, the axes always span from 0 to 1 in a particular coordinate system.

Also, by changing xmin to 0.5, we get the following:

```
# Span Axis coverage (min/max)
nums = np.arange(0,10,0.1)
plt.plot(nums, np.sin(nums))
plt.axhspan(-0.5,0.5, xmin=0.5, xmax=1, alpha=0.5)
```

We will get the following output:

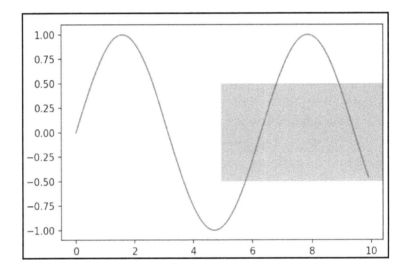

Also, by changing xmax to 0.75, we get:

```
# Span Axis coverage (min/max)
nums = np.arange(0,10,0.1)
plt.plot(nums, np.sin(nums))
plt.axhspan(-0.5,0.5, xmin=0.5, xmax=0.75, alpha=0.5)
```

We will get the following output:

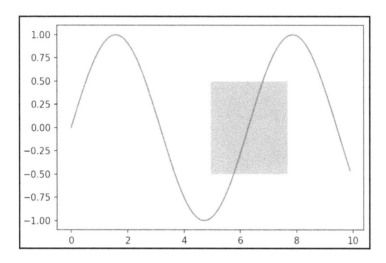

This is a quick and easy way to highlight particular points of your data that you want to show to the viewer.

Adding and tweaking a background grid

We can also apply a background grid. It will lay down gridlines, which will show the reader and the viewer that each of the ticks extends far away from the axis. This is often useful if you want the viewer to be able to draw direct numerical values by looking at pieces of the grid or of their plot. So, it's important for your viewer to be able to actually look at a point or a piece of a line and draw out the numerical value of the grid lines, as shown here:

```
# Gridlines
nums = np.arange(0,10,0.1)
plt.plot(nums, np.sin(nums))
plt.grid()
```

We will get the following output:

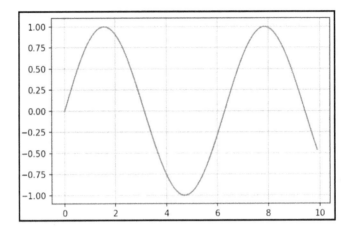

Like any other set of lines in Matplotlib, we have a number of different attributes that we can give to these grids.

We can color them, so you can change them to red, as shown here:

```
# Gridlines
nums = np.arange(0,10,0.1)
plt.plot(nums, np.sin(nums))
plt.grid(color='r')
```

We will get the following output:

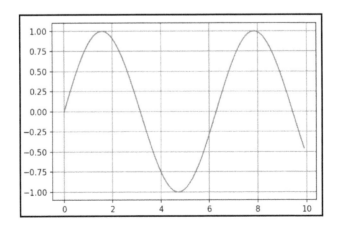

We can also change the line style. By default, we can see it's solid in the preceding diagram. But this can be changed easily into dotted lines, as shown here:

```
# Gridlines
nums = np.arange(0,10,0.1)
plt.plot(nums, np.sin(nums))
plt.grid(color='r', linestyle='--')
```

We will get the following output:

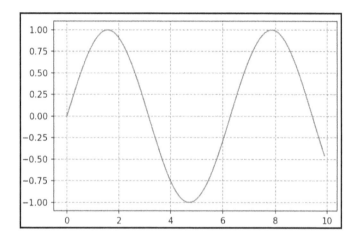

Hence, if the dotted line is not the aesthetic appearance that the user wants, we can change that quite easily, and any of the other attributes that we have seen for tweaking the appearance of lines can be applied to this grid.

Adding text on your plots

This section describes how we can add text to both the axis and figure objects, including adding text in multi-panel figures and configuring the appearance of text.

Adding text to both axis and figure objects

Let's start by importing everything we need:

```
import numpy as np
import matplotlib as mpl
import matplotlib.pyplot as plt
```

```
%matplotlib inline
# Set up figure size and DPI for screen demo
plt.rcParams['figure.figsize'] = (6,4)
plt.rcParams['figure.dpi'] = 150
```

1. Next, bring up the standard sine curve that we have been using:

    ```
    # Add some text
    nums = np.arange(0,10,0.1)
    plt.plot(nums, np.sin(nums))
    ```

    We will get the following output:

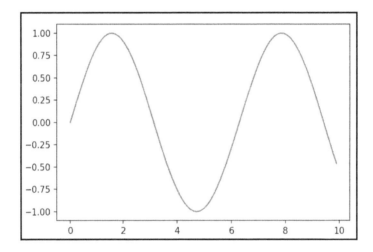

2. We will add some text, say, right in the middle of the two curves. We will use the text method, and since we are taking the data coordinates, the middle of this plot would be (5, 0), so the arguments here are the X and Y coordinates, and then the text that you want to display would be seen as follows:

    ```
    # Add some text
    nums = np.arange(0,10,0.1)
    plt.plot(nums, np.sin(nums))
    plt.text(5,0, "sine curve")
    ```

    The output can be seen as follows:

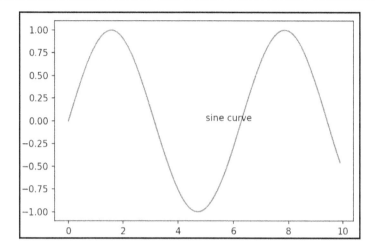

But the preceding output does not look centered. In fact, from the preceding output, it's putting the beginning of our text at (5, 0).

3. To get this centered, we will use the horizontal alignment keyword argument (by default, it's set to left). When changing it to center, we will see it then looks a lot more centered:

```
# Horizontal alignment
nums = np.arange(0,10,0.1)
plt.plot(nums, np.sin(nums))
plt.text(5, 0, "sine curve", horizontalalignment='center')
```

We get the output as follows:

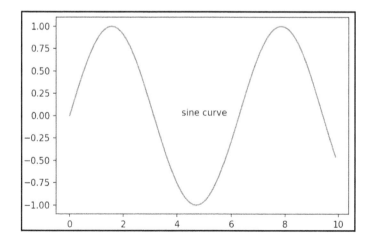

4. You can also choose `'right'`, as shown:

```
# Horizontal alignment
nums = np.arange(0,10,0.1)
plt.plot(nums, np.sin(nums))
plt.text(5, 0, "sine curve", horizontalalignment='right')
```

The output can be shown as follows:

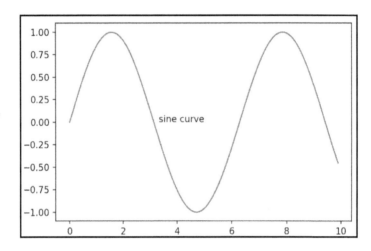

5. You can also change the font size by passing the `size` keyword argument that can take a size in points. We will insert the `size` as `18` for the pointer:

```
# Font size
nums = np.arange(0,10,0.1)
plt.plot(nums, np.sin(nums))
plt.text(5, 0, "sine curve", size=18)
```

We will get the following output:

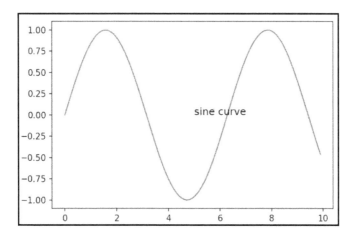

6. For a small size keyword, insert the following:

```
# Font size
nums = np.arange(0,10,0.1)
plt.plot(nums, np.sin(nums))
plt.text(5, 0, "sine curve", size=8)
```

The output can be seen as follows:

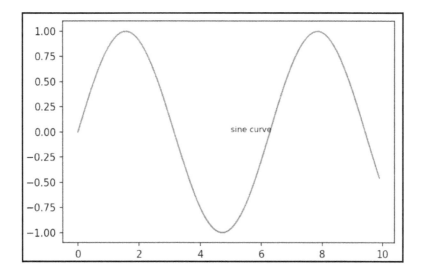

7. We can pass a large font size:

```
# Font size
nums = np.arange(0,10,0.1)
plt.plot(nums, np.sin(nums))
plt.text(5, 0, "sine curve", size='large')
```

We will get the following output:

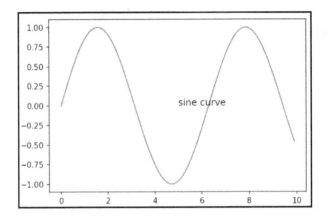

8. For an extra-large font size, use the following:

```
# Font size
nums = np.arange(0,10,0.1)
plt.plot(nums, np.sin(nums))
plt.text(5, 0, "sine curve", size='x-large')
```

The output can be seen as follows:

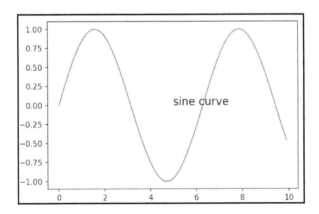

9. For a double-extra-large font, use the following code:

```
# Font size
nums = np.arange(0,10,0.1)
plt.plot(nums, np.sin(nums))
plt.text(5, 0, "sine curve", size='xx-large')
```

We will get the following output:

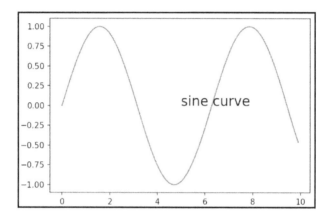

This is often nice if you want figures that you can change to the actual figure size without having to worry about going in and then tweaking all of the font sizes.

10. There are also a number of different keyword arguments to tweak the appearance of your fonts, including the family keyword arguments. So, by passing monospace, we will get a monospace font, as shown here:

```
# Font family, weight & style
nums = np.arange(0,10,0.1)
plt.plot(nums, np.sin(nums))
plt.text(5, 0, "sine curve", family='monospace')
```

The output for the preceding code can be seen as follows:

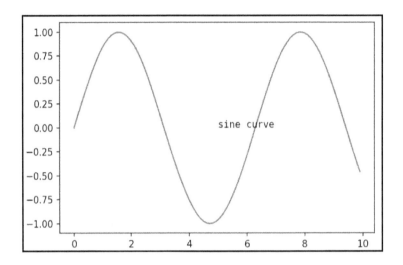

11. There's also the `serif` font if you want a Roman style font:

```
# Font family, weight & style
nums = np.arange(0,10,0.1)
plt.plot(nums, np.sin(nums))
plt.text(5, 0, "sine curve", family='serif')
```

We will get the following output:

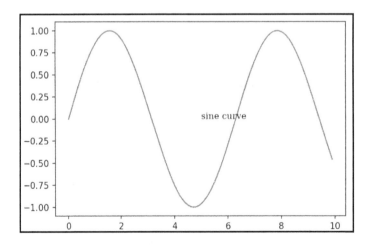

12. You also have the ability to take a look at the weight by passing bold and getting a `bold` style:

```
# Font family, weight & style
nums = np.arange(0,10,0.1)
plt.plot(nums, np.sin(nums))
plt.text(5, 0, "sine curve", weight='bold')
```

We will get the output as follows:

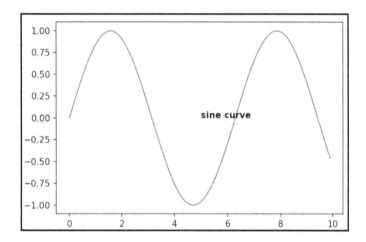

13. We also have the style font. For example, to get an italic font, we pass `style='italic'`:

```
# Font family, weight & style
nums = np.arange(0,10,0.1)
plt.plot(nums, np.sin(nums))
plt.text(5, 0, "sine curve", style='italic')
```

The following output is as follows:

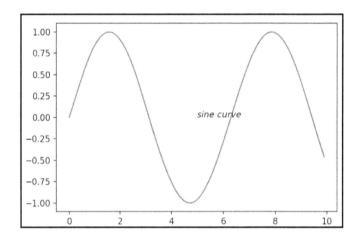

14. Often, we want this curve to point by using two keyword arguments, `withdash=True` and `dashlength=24`. We will add a little dash, as shown here:

```
# Adding dash withdash & dashlength
nums = np.arange(0,10,0.1)
plt.plot(nums, np.sin(nums))
plt.text(5, 0, "sine curve", withdash=True, dashlength=24)
```

We will get the following output:

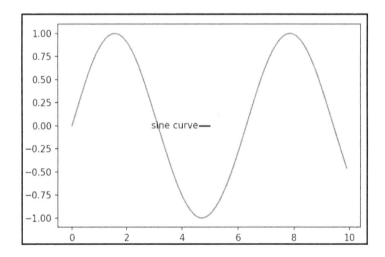

15. By changing the data coordinates to `(6, 0)`, we get a nice little dash pointing at the curve:

```
# Adding dash withdash & dashlength
nums = np.arange(0,10,0.1)
plt.plot(nums, np.sin(nums))
plt.text(6, 0, "sine curve", withdash=True, dashlength=24)
```

We get the following output from the preceding code:

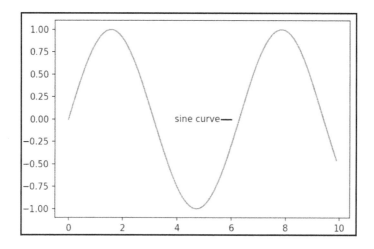

In further sections, we will take a look at a much more versatile way of adding little dashes and arrows.

You can also pass a keyword argument that will rotate your text, so if we have to rotate the text by 45 degrees, pass `rotation = 45` and it will rotate on this axis, so depending on what your horizontal alignment is, it will rotate around the `(5,0)` point. This could mean that the text is rotated about the center or it could mean that the text is rotated about one of the edges, as shown here:

```
# Rotating text
nums = np.arange(0,10,0.1)
plt.plot(nums, np.sin(nums))
plt.text(5, 0, "sine curve", rotation=45)
```

We will get the following output:

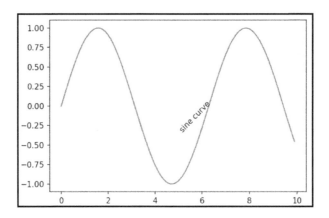

To add multiple lines, for example, if we want the word `sine` on top of the word `curve`, we need to put a newline character in the string. Since that's escaped, we would want to put an `r` to allow the literal, as shown here:

```
# Multi line
nums = np.arange(0,10,0.1)
plt.plot(nums, np.sin(nums))
plt.text(5, 0, "sine\ncurve")
```

The output is shown as follows:

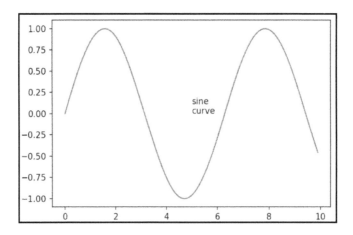

Adding text in multi-panel figures

This section describes how to align our text and put it on the figure object rather than the axis objects.

The following is the code for the two-axis figure, with a sine curve and a cosine curve seperated by spine:

```
# Figure text
gs = mpl.gridspec.GridSpec(1,2, wspace=0.0)
nums = np.arange(0,10,0.1)
plt.subplot(gs[0])
plt.plot(nums, np.sin(nums))
plt.gca().spines['right'].set_visible(False)
plt.gca().yaxis.set_ticks_position('left')
plt.subplot(gs[1])
plt.plot(nums, np.cos(nums))
# plt.gca().yaxis.set_visible(False)
# plt.gca().spines['left'].set_visible(False)
plt.gca().xaxis.set_major_locator(mpl.ticker.MaxNLocator(5, prune='lower'))
# plt.figtext(0.5,0.5, "trig functions", horizontalalignment='center')
```

To span the text in this multiple panel plot, as shown in the following output, we will have to following some steps:

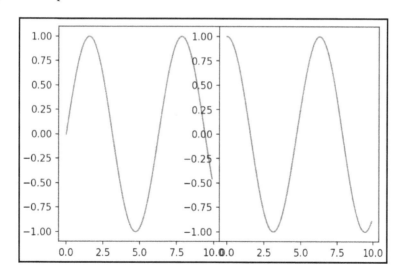

1. Start by disabling the spine in the middle, so here we have a two-axis figure with a sine curve and a cosine curve:

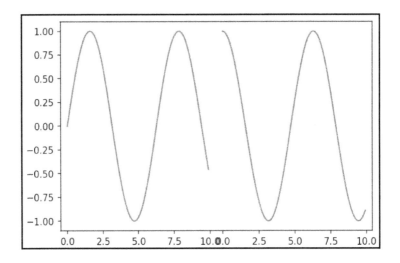

2. If we want to annotate this figure, we will use the figtext method; figtext takes the figure coordinate system. To give an example of what that does, when we pass trig functions as the string, it takes the same three kinds of arguments—x, y, and then the string. In fact, it is outside of the axes limits, as shown here:

```
# Figure text
gs = mpl.gridspec.GridSpec(1,2, wspace=0.0)
nums = np.arange(0,10,0.1)
plt.subplot(gs[0])
plt.plot(nums, np.sin(nums))
plt.gca().spines['right'].set_visible(False)
plt.gca().yaxis.set_ticks_position('left')
plt.subplot(gs[1])
plt.plot(nums, np.cos(nums))
plt.gca().yaxis.set_visible(False)
plt.gca().spines['left'].set_visible(False)
plt.gca().xaxis.set_major_locator(mpl.ticker.MaxNLocator(5,
prune='lower'))
plt.figtext(0,0, "trig functions")
```

We will get the following output:

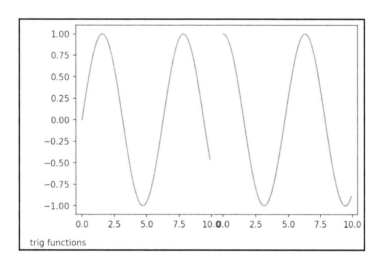

3. To place this right in the middle, we can pass (0.5, 0.5). To get it centered, we will use horizontalalignment='center':

```
# Figure text
gs = mpl.gridspec.GridSpec(1,2, wspace=0.0)
nums = np.arange(0,10,0.1)
plt.subplot(gs[0])
plt.plot(nums, np.sin(nums))
plt.gca().spines['right'].set_visible(False)
plt.gca().yaxis.set_ticks_position('left')
plt.subplot(gs[1])
plt.plot(nums, np.cos(nums))
plt.gca().yaxis.set_visible(False)
plt.gca().spines['left'].set_visible(False)
plt.gca().xaxis.set_major_locator(mpl.ticker.MaxNLocator(5,
prune='lower'))
plt.figtext(0.5,0.5, "trig functions",
horizontalalignment='center')
```

We get the texts anchored to the very middle of this multi-panel figure, as shown here:

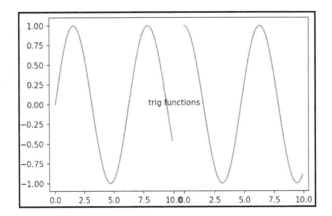

So, for multi-panel plots, `figtext` is to be used, and for single-panel plots, we will use the text so that it's anchored to the figure coordinates rather than to the data coordinates.

Hence, in order to place the text in the center of the plot, we are not sure about the data axes; the figure text is the tool to be used to place the text at the center.

Playing with polygons and shapes

This section talks about how to add polygons and other shapes and the different built-in shapes that Matplotlib provides.

Adding polygons and shapes to our plots

We will begin by importing what we need to from Matplotlib, as shown here:

```
import numpy as np
import matplotlib as mpl
import matplotlib.pyplot as plt
%matplotlib inline
# Set up figure size and DPI for screen demo
plt.rcParams['figure.figsize'] = (6,4)
plt.rcParams['figure.dpi'] = 150
nums = np.arange(0,10,0.1)
plt.plot(nums, np.sin(nums))
```

We will use the same sign plot as in the earlier section, *Adding text to both axis and figure objects*. As shown in the following output, this is the most basic sine plot and no annotations have been added yet:

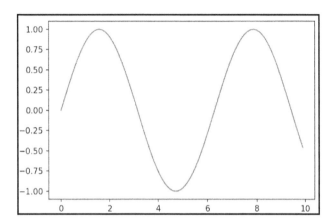

Begin by adding a circle in-between them. Define the circle using the Matplotlib patches module, as shown here:

```
# Circle
circ = mpl.patches.Circle((5,0), radius=1)
plt.plot(nums, np.sin(nums))
plt.gca().add_patch(circ)
```

We get a circle with a radius of one, as shown here:

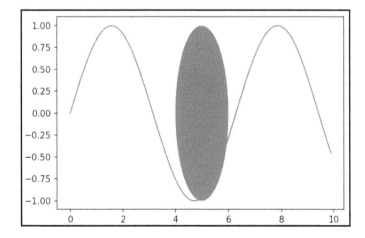

The preceding figure does not look exactly like a circle; it looks like an ellipse that has been stretched—this is because our axis does not have an equal aspect ratio, even though it ranges from + 1 to -1.

To get the aspect ratio to be equal, we use the set_aspect method on the axis objects. If we set this to be equal, the *x* and *y* coordinates actually map an equal ratio to the data or to the size of the figure itself, so that we get a much longer looking plot, but our circle actually becomes circular, as follows:

```
# Circle
circ = mpl.patches.Circle((5,0), radius=1)
plt.plot(nums, np.sin(nums))
plt.gca().add_patch(circ)
plt.gca().set_aspect('equal')
```

We will get the following output:

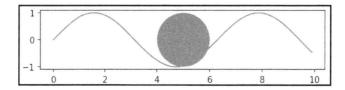

 If you're wondering why the polygons and the shapes that you've added to your plot don't look exactly like you expect them to, keep in mind that the aspect ratios may not always be equal by default.

We can add two patches to a plot by performing the following function:

```
# zorder
c1 = mpl.patches.Circle((5,0), radius=1)
c2 = mpl.patches.Circle((4,0), radius=1, color='r')
plt.plot(nums, 10/3.*np.sin(nums))
plt.gca().add_patch(c1)
plt.gca().add_patch(c2)
```

We will get the following output:

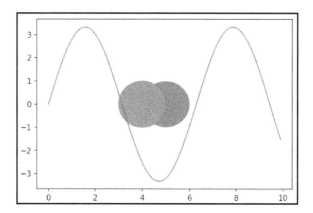

In the preceding figure, we have two circles; the above circle is the one that was added last to the axis, and the circle that's below is the one that was added first.

When we swap the order (for specification you can add colors to the circles to distinguish them) we will see that the circles will be overlapped, as shown:

```
# zorder
c1 = mpl.patches.Circle((5,0), radius=1)
c2 = mpl.patches.Circle((4,0), radius=1, color='r')
plt.plot(nums, 10/3.*np.sin(nums))
plt.gca().add_patch(c2)
plt.gca().add_patch(c1)
```

The output can be shown as:

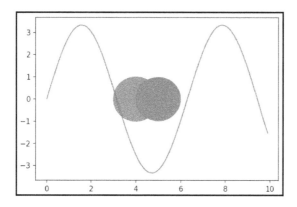

But if you have multiple patches, or multiple shapes, or polygons, it is not necessary to overlap them simply based on the order they're called in. To set this manually, we can use the `zorder` argument. The object with the highest `zorder` is the one that is displayed last – it's the one that ends up overlapping all of the rest.

So, if we set the first one to have a `zorder` of 0 and the second one to have a `zorder` of 1, the second one will be the one on top, as shown here:

```
# zorder
c1 = mpl.patches.Circle((5,0), radius=1, zorder=0)
c2 = mpl.patches.Circle((4,0), radius=1, zorder=1, color='r')
```

We get the following screenshot:

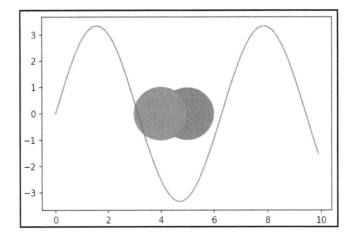

If the zorders are swapped, in which the second one has the `zorder` of 0 and the first one has the `zorder` of 1, the first one will be the one on top, as shown here:

```
# zorder
c1 = mpl.patches.Circle((5,0), radius=1, zorder=1)
c2 = mpl.patches.Circle((4,0), radius=1, zorder=0, color='r')
plt.plot(nums, 10/3.*np.sin(nums))
plt.gca().add_patch(c2)
plt.gca().add_patch(c1)
```

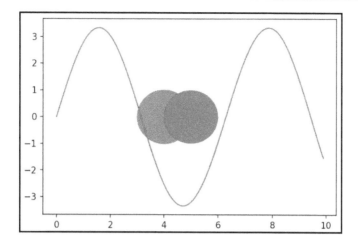

Hence, whichever patch has the highest `zorder` will be the one that is drawn last. So, if you want to set what covers other patches, keep in mind that the `zorder` is the best way of doing this; otherwise, we can simply use the order in which they are added to the plot.

The built-in shapes that Matplotlib provides

There are a lot of different kinds of patches available, beyond just the simple circle. They are as follows:

- The circle, in which you can set the center and the radius.
- An arc, which is an elliptical arc, that takes a section of an ellipse that you specify using the width and the height. We can also change the angle that that ellipse is placed at and then, using a pair of angles, theta 1 and theta 2, we set how much of that ellipse is filled.
- A wedge, wherein we get an additional argument, called the **width**, which explains what fraction of that circle will be shown.
- An arrow, which specifies the position of the tail using the *x* and *y* coordinates and where that arrow will point using `dx` and `dy`. So, these will point in a vector away from the tail.
- There is also a filled ellipse, which includes width, height, and angle.
- A filled rectangle.
- An arbitrary polygon where we set the center, the number of vertices, the orientation, and the radius.

We will take a look at all of the patches:

```
# Different kinds of simple patches
circle = mpl.patches.Circle(xy=(2,-2), radius=1)
arc = mpl.patches.Arc(xy=(1,2), width=1, height=3, angle=0, theta1=90,
theta2=270)
wedge = mpl.patches.Wedge(center=(2,2), r=1, theta1=-180, theta2=100,
width=0.5)
arrow = mpl.patches.Arrow(x=4,y=-3, dx=2, dy=2)
ellipse = mpl.patches.Ellipse(xy=(5,2), width=1, height=3, angle=60)
rect = mpl.patches.Rectangle(xy=(7,-2), width=2, height=2, angle=-30)
poly = mpl.patches.RegularPolygon(xy=(8,2), numVertices=3, orientation=45,
radius=1)
plt.plot(nums, 10/3.*np.sin(nums))
plt.gca().add_patch(circle)
plt.gca().add_patch(arc)
plt.gca().add_patch(wedge)
plt.gca().add_patch(arrow)
plt.gca().add_patch(ellipse)
plt.gca().add_patch(rect)
plt.gca().add_patch(poly)
```

In the following output, we have a circle, an arc, a wedge that is partially filled in, an ellipse, an arrow, a polygon, and a rectangle:

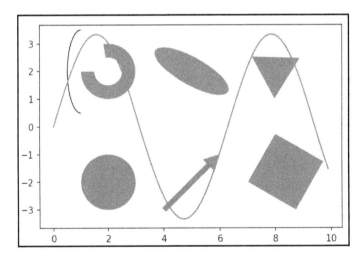

Now, you can probably already guess from this that a circle is more or less a special case of an ellipse, and a rectangle is more or less a special case of polygons. So, you can, in many cases, only get away with using a ellipse and polygon instead of a circle and rectangle, but there are a few cases where it makes sense to use the more explicit way of doing things.

Building your own polygons

You can also make your own polygons by specifying where those vertices lie. In the following code, we can see that there are four vertices corresponding to a trapezoid, as follows:

```
# Making your own polygons
pos = [(3,0),(7,0), (6,1), (4,1)]
poly = mpl.patches.Polygon(pos)
plt.plot(nums, 10/3.*np.sin(nums))
plt.gca().add_patch(poly)
```

When we run this code, we get a trapezoid, as shown here:

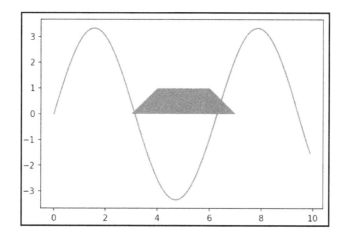

Matplotlib provides the ability to build much more complicated and sophisticated shapes using paths. It is recommended to take a look at the `matplotlib.path` module. In the `path` module, we can see that there is a module available for dealing with multiple different kinds of lines. By combining these different lines—straight lines, Bezier curves, and other lines—we can build any kind of shape that we want:

```
mpl.path?
```

We will get the following screen:

```
Type:          module
String form: <module 'matplotlib.path' from 'C:\\Users\\sagarsawant\\AppData\\Local\\Continuum\\Anaconda3\\anaconda\\lib
\\site-packages\\matplotlib\\path.py'>
File:          ~\appdata\local\continuum\anaconda3\anaconda\lib\site-packages\matplotlib\path.py
Docstring:
A module for dealing with the polylines used throughout matplotlib.

The primary class for polyline handling in matplotlib is :class:`Path`.
Almost all vector drawing makes use of Paths somewhere in the drawing
pipeline.

Whilst a :class:`Path` instance itself cannot be drawn, there exists
:class:`~matplotlib.artist.Artist` subclasses which can be used for
convenient Path visualisation - the two most frequently used of these are
:class:`~matplotlib.patches.PathPatch` and
:class:`~matplotlib.collections.PathCollection`.
```

In fact, Matplotlib provides a language similar to SVG, where we can build sophisticated vector graphics.

Versatile annotating

We will import everything we need to bring up the simple sine plot:

```
import numpy as np
import matplotlib as mpl
import matplotlib.pyplot as plt
%matplotlib inline
# Set up figure size and DPI for screen demo
plt.rcParams['figure.figsize'] = (6,4)
plt.rcParams['figure.dpi'] = 150
```

Adding arrows to our plots with the annotate method

The `annotate` method has a lot of arguments, as seen in the following code:

```
# Add an arrow
nums = np.arange(0,10,0.1)
plt.plot(nums, np.sin(nums))
plt.annotate("", xy=(np.pi/2, 1), xytext=(5,0),
arrowprops=dict(facecolor='k'))
```

The first argument in the preceding code is an empty string that will be displayed. `xy` tells us where the data coordinates are placed, which is the head. `xytext` tells us where the text of the tail of the arrow will be placed and the `arrowprops` argument explains without specifying a color for the arrow—it only uses text that will be displayed. We will start by looking at the arrow itself since we already know how to add text.

As you can see in the following output, we get a nice black arrow. The tip of it is at PI over (2, 1), pointing at the first peak of our sine curve and the tail of it is at (5, 0), where we want our `xytext`:

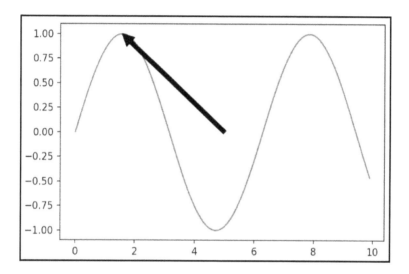

Adding some text to the arrows

We will add some text under the arrow, as shown in the following points:

1. Change the empty string to a string that says `1st peak`:

```
# Add text
nums = np.arange(0,10,0.1)
plt.plot(nums, np.sin(nums))
plt.annotate("1st peak", xy=(np.pi/2, 1), xytext=(5,0),
arrowprops=dict(facecolor='k'))
```

We will thus get some text that begins at `(5, 0)`, and the tip of our arrow pointing at PI over `(2, 1)`:

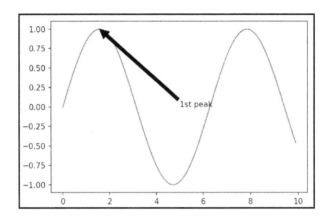

2. This text takes all of the usual keyword arguments that the text method itself takes, so we will include `color= red`, `weight =bold`, `style=italic`, and all of those will be passed on, as follows:

```
# Customize text
nums = np.arange(0,10,0.1)
plt.plot(nums, np.sin(nums))
plt.annotate("look!", xy=(np.pi/2, 1), xytext=(5,0), color='red',
weight='bold', style='italic', arrowprops=dict(facecolor='k'))
```

Here, we get a nice, bold, italic text, as follows:

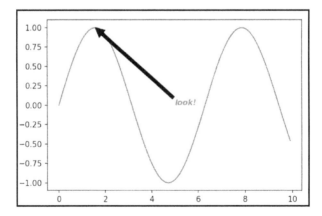

3. The arrow itself is customized with `arrowprops=dict`, so, for example, when we pass `shrink=0.5`, we cut off the bottom half of the arrow, as shown here:

```
# Customize the arrow (width, headwidth, headlength, shrink)
nums = np.arange(0,10,0.1)
plt.plot(nums, np.sin(nums))
plt.annotate("look!", xy=(np.pi/2, 1), xytext=(5,0),
arrowprops=dict(facecolor='k', headwidth=50, headlength=40,
shrink=0.5))
```

We get the following output:

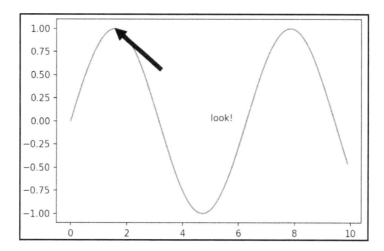

4. For a wide arrow with a width of ten, insert `width=10`, and we get the following output:

```
# Customize the arrow (width, headwidth, headlength, shrink)
nums = np.arange(0,10,0.1)
plt.plot(nums, np.sin(nums))
plt.annotate("look!", xy=(np.pi/2, 1), xytext=(5,0),
arrowprops=dict(facecolor='k', width=10, shrink=0.5))
```

The output can be seen as follows:

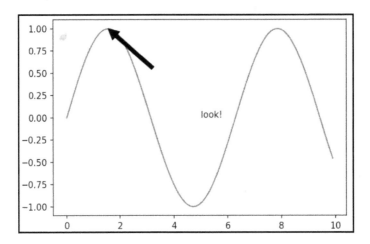

5. For changing the width of the head argument, include `headwidth=50`—there, you can see that the head of the arrow gets very big:

```
# Customize the arrow (width, headwidth, headlength, shrink)
nums = np.arange(0,10,0.1)
plt.plot(nums, np.sin(nums))
plt.annotate("look!", xy=(np.pi/2, 1), xytext=(5,0),
arrowprops=dict(facecolor='k', headwidth=50, shrink=0.5))
```

We get the following output:

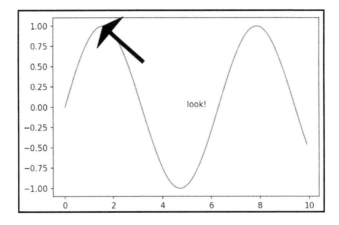

6. The length of the head can also be changed, so the head itself is manipulated with these keyword arguments, as shown here:

```
# Customize the arrow (width, headwidth, headlength, shrink)
nums = np.arange(0,10,0.1)
plt.plot(nums, np.sin(nums))
plt.annotate("look!", xy=(np.pi/2, 1), xytext=(5,0),
arrowprops=dict(facecolor='k', headwidth=50, headlength=40,
shrink=0.5))
```

We get the following output:

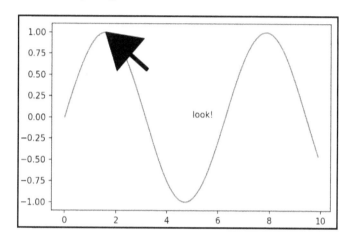

7. There is also an ability to pass different kinds of arrow styles. By default, the arrow style key is not passed in `arrowprops=dict`—it will use `arrowstyle='simple'`, as shown in the following code:

```
# Customize the arrow (arrowstyles with attributes)
nums = np.arange(0,10,0.1)
plt.plot(nums, np.sin(nums))
plt.annotate("look!", xy=(np.pi/2, 1), xytext=(5,0),
arrowprops=dict(arrowstyle='simple'))
```

We get the following output:

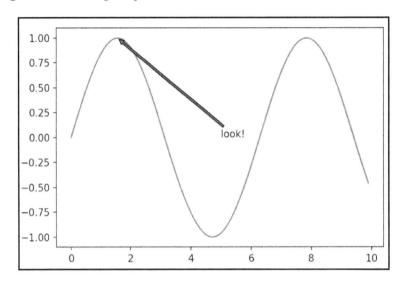

8. We can also have a fancy arrow that gives a wedge, as shown here:

```
# Customize the arrow (arrowstyles with attributes)
nums = np.arange(0,10,0.1)
plt.plot(nums, np.sin(nums))
plt.annotate("look!", xy=(np.pi/2, 1), xytext=(5,0),
arrowprops=dict(arrowstyle='fancy'))
```

We get the following output:

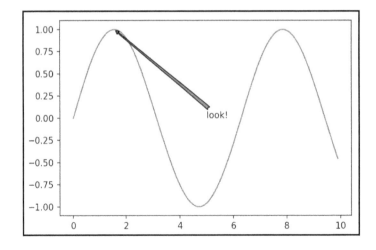

9. Series punctuation can be included to make simpler line-type arrows, as shown here:

```
# Customize the arrow (arrowstyles with attributes)
nums = np.arange(0,10,0.1)
plt.plot(nums, np.sin(nums))
plt.annotate("look!", xy=(np.pi/2, 1), xytext=(5,0),
arrowprops=dict(arrowstyle='->'))
```

We get the following output:

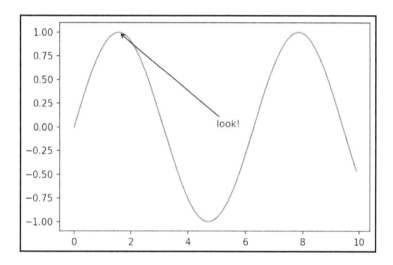

10. Also, flat edges can be added in order to show distance, as shown here:

```
# Customize the arrow (arrowstyles with attributes)
nums = np.arange(0,10,0.1)
plt.plot(nums, np.sin(nums))
plt.annotate("look!", xy=(np.pi/2, 1), xytext=(5,0),
arrowprops=dict(arrowstyle='|-|'))
```

The output can be seen as follows:

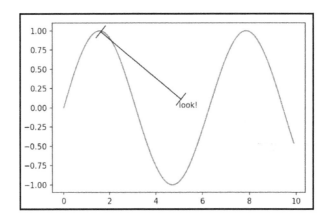

11. We can also include boxy edges, as shown in the following code:

```
# Customize the arrow (arrowstyles with attributes)
nums = np.arange(0,10,0.1)
plt.plot(nums, np.sin(nums))
plt.annotate("look!", xy=(np.pi/2, 1), xytext=(5,0),
arrowprops=dict(arrowstyle=']-['))
```

We get the following output:

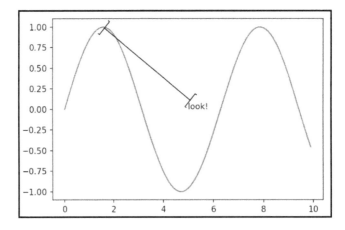

Customizing the appearance of the annotations

There are many different options available to annotate a particular region.

1. We can also pass arrow-style attributes. So, if we insert `head_length=2` and `head_width=2`, we get the following output:

```
# Customize the arrow (arrowstyles with attributes)
nums = np.arange(0,10,0.1)
plt.plot(nums, np.sin(nums))
plt.annotate("look!", xy=(np.pi/2, 1), xytext=(5,0),
arrowprops=dict(arrowstyle='fancy,head_length=2,head_width=2'))
```

The preceding code gives us the following output:

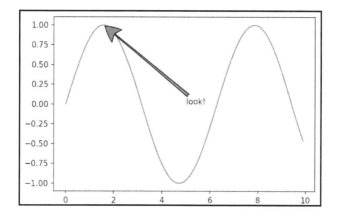

So far, we have been looking at very straight arrows—with annotate, we have the ability to actually curve these arrows along arcs. This is very useful as it helps to guide the viewer's eye, not just to the tips where we have the text and the head, but along the plot as well.

2. Hence, often, if we want to annotate things that also show flow or curve, we could curve the arrow. We will insert 0.5, which gives a curve at an angle of 0.5 radians, as shown here:

```
# Customize the arrow (connectionstyle w/ angle3, arc3)
nums = np.arange(0,10,0.1)
plt.plot(nums, np.sin(nums))
plt.annotate("look!", xy=(np.pi/2, 1), xytext=(5,0),
arrowprops=dict(arrowstyle='fancy',
connectionstyle='arc3,rad=0.5'))
```

The output can be shown as follows:

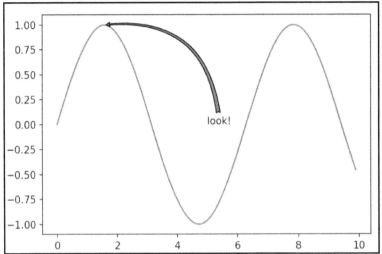

When we insert the `angle3` option, it takes two keyword arguments: `angleA` and `angleB`.

 As can be seen in the following figure, these angles do not come in as separate keys; they come after commas in the string.

3. These angles, unlike for `arc3`, are in degrees, so they describe the angle at the tip and the angle at the text:

```
# Customize the arrow (connectionstyle w/ angle3, arc3)
nums = np.arange(0,10,0.1)
plt.plot(nums, np.sin(nums))
plt.annotate("look!", xy=(np.pi/2, 1), xytext=(5,0),
arrowprops=dict(arrowstyle='fancy',
 connectionstyle='angle3,angleA=-30,angleB=30'))
```

Hence here, we can see the twist in the arrow:

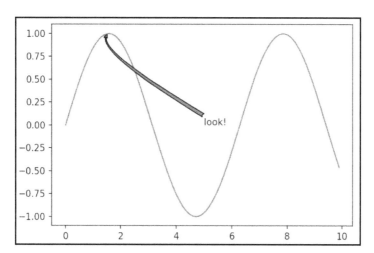

We often find that parts of the plot are covered up by the arrow annotation. If we want to show the curve of some other part of the data, we can use `angle3` or `arc3` as a quick and easy way of doing that.

Summary

In this chapter, we learned how to add lines, boxes, texts, different kinds of shapes, and polygons, as well as arrows in descriptions with annotate. We also focused on the viewer's attention on whatever kinds of data the plot is showing to make the insights.

In the next chapter, we will learn about special-purpose plots, which you can use for different kinds of data that haven't fallen into the sorts of plots we've seen so far.

3
Special Purpose Plots

We have so far learned how to add lines, boxes, texts, different kinds of shapes, as well as arrows in descriptions with annotation. Special purpose plots defines how to draw on plots to provide the viewer with visual guides that point them toward the important features of data and a few special purpose kinds of plots for either plotting non-Cartesian data or very specific kinds of datasets.

In this chapter, we will learn about the following topics:

- How to make non-Cartesian axes and plots
- How to plot vector fields
- How to show statistical information with box and violin plots
- How to display ordinal and tabular data

Non-Cartesian plots

We will begin by importing all the necessary packages, as follows:

```
import numpy as np
import matplotlib as mpl
import matplotlib.pyplot as plt
%matplotlib inline
# Set up figure size and DPI for screen demo
plt.rcParams['figure.figsize'] = (6,4)
plt.rcParams['figure.dpi'] = 150
```

Creating polar axes

First, we will bring up a simple plot with the following code:

```
nums = np.arange(0,10,0.1)
plt.plot(nums, nums/10.)
plt.plot(nums, np.sin(nums))
plt.plot(nums, np.cos(nums))
```

The preceding code will give the following output:

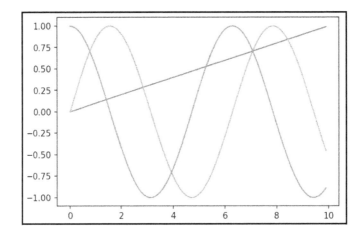

The preceding output shows a sine and cosine plot, with a linear plot alongside it. We will take a look at the cosine and sine plot, but not as a function of its linear length. Instead, we will interpret it in which sine and cosine are used mathematically, namely regarding their trigonometric functions, which deal with angles. The numbers that we are passing to sine and cosine can be interpreted as angles, with the sine being the opposite length of a given angle and the cosine being the adjacent side's length. Often, while dealing with trigonometric or harmonic data where one of our axes is similar to that of an angle, we will take a look at it in a bowler projection and actually treat it like an angle.

We will bring up a subplot and insert `111`, giving the `projection='polar'` keyword argument alongside it, as follows:

```
nums = np.arange(0,10,0.1)
plt.subplot(111, projection='polar')
plt.plot(nums, nums/10.)
plt.plot(nums, np.sin(nums))
plt.plot(nums, np.cos(nums))
```

The output of the preceding code is as follows:

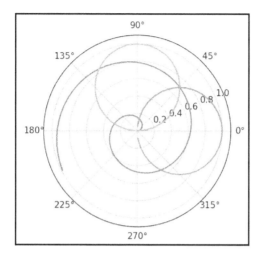

In the preceding output, we get a polar plot where the values are treated as actual radians. We can see that the sine curve is looking at the positive parts of the triangle and that it resides in the upper half of our polar plot. The cosine curve resides in the right half of our polar plot and the linear curve. While traveling from 0 to 10, we can see that the curve is actually multivalued in a lot of places, so at the 0 angle, there are two points. Often, a polar plot can be visually informative in such a way that a Cartesian plot is not necessary.

Applying log, symmetric log, and logistic scales to your axes

To apply log, symmetric log and logistic scales we will go through the steps as follows:

1. Plot the numbers from 0 to 10 against the power of 10, as shown:

```
# Log axes
plt.plot(nums, np.power(10,10*nums))
plt.gca().grid(True)
```

Following is the output of the preceding code:

In the preceding output, we can see that the plot is not very good for actually viewing these numbers, since the end of the data range is much bigger than the beginning of the data range.

2. We can transform this into something that will fill the space, so that we are not left with an empty space, by using an algorithm. The easiest way to do this is to remove the `plot` keyword and call `semilogy`, as follows:

```
# Log axes
plt.semilogy(nums, np.power(10,10*nums))
plt.gca().grid(True)
```

The output of the preceding code is as follows:

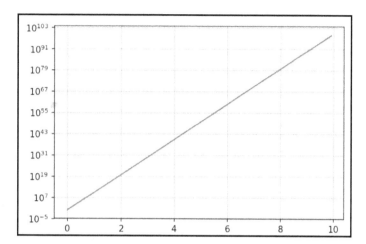

In the preceding output, we can see the logarithm of the numbers and a perfectly straight line since the logarithm of the exponent is an identity.

3. We can also get the logs for both axes by using plt.loglog. By doing this, we have a much better way of visualizing this information:

```
# Log axes
plt.loglog(nums, np.power(10,10*nums))
plt.gca().grid(True)
```

Following is the output of the preceding code:

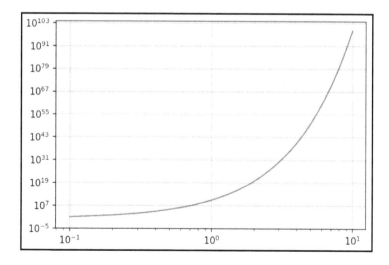

4. The scale can also be changed by using the `set_yscale` method, as shown in the following code:

```
# Log axes
plt.plot(nums, np.power(10,10*nums))
plt.gca().set_yscale('log')
plt.gca().grid(True)
```

We will get the following output:

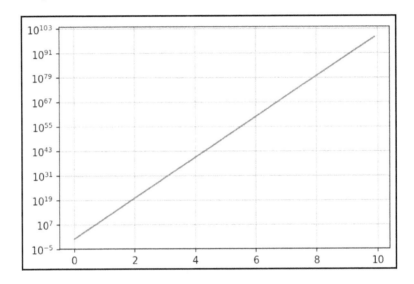

For self-learning, you can use the `set_xscale` method, which will give a different output.

5. Taking another example, in the following output, we have a wide range of data. Again, most of it looks like a straight line because the end is so much bigger than the beginning:

```
# Symlog axes
plt.plot(nums, np.power(10,nums)-100)
plt.gca().grid(True)
```

Following is the output of the preceding code:

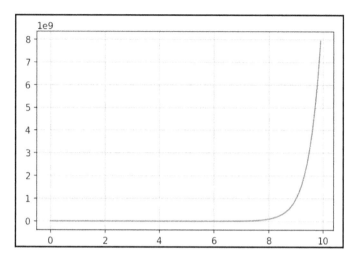

6. Looking at the `log`, we get the following:

```
# Symlog axes
plt.plot(nums, np.power(10,nums)-100)
plt.gca().set_yscale('log')
plt.gca().grid(True)
```

We will get the following output:

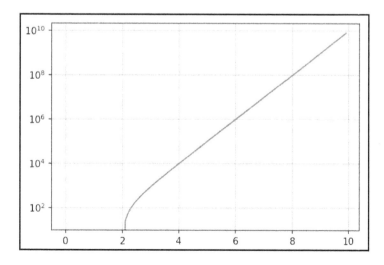

7. For this case, where we have some negative and positive values and a huge dynamic range, Matplotlib provides the `symlog` scale, which actually splits into two log plots, one showing the positive values and the other showing the negative values. This is a nice way to actually visualize stuff that has a huge dynamic range and still contains a mixture of positive and negative values:

```
# Symlog axes
plt.plot(nums, np.power(10,nums)-100)
plt.gca().set_yscale('symlog')
plt.gca().grid(True)
```

Following is the output of the preceding code:

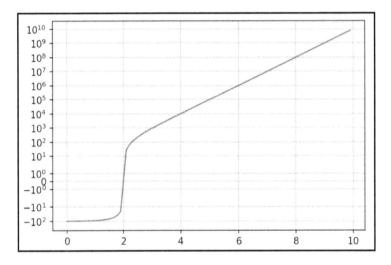

Finally, Matplotlib provides a third linear scale called the logistic or logit axis scale.

We have values between 0 and 1. Logistic scales are really good for dealing with probabilities. If there are probabilities that have mostly 0s in some places but peak up toward 1, you want to be able to visualize this more easily—the logistic or logit axis is really good for that.

8. The one downside with the logistic axis are not well-scaled, so they tend to run right into each other, as shown here:

```
# Logistic axes
plt.plot(nums, nums/10)
plt.gca().set_yscale('logit')
plt.gca().grid(True)
# plt.gca().yaxis.set_minor_formatter(mpl.ticker.NullFormatter())
```

The preceding code gives the following output:

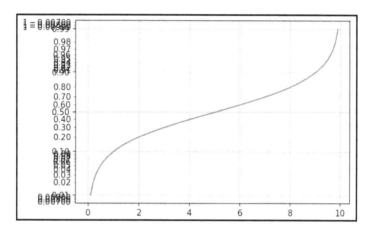

As we can see, the logistic axis gives a lot of information on the left and right-hand sides. It focuses at the resolution – we can think of it like a map projection where it is focusing on the amount of space at the high and low ends, around 0 and 1.

Hence, while dealing with this kind of scale, we have to get rid of the jumbled up values that are present on the *y* axis by disabling the formatter for the minor axis. By doing this, it keeps the ticks. They are often useful to see, and won't have that ugly mashup of text.

Plotting vector fields

First, though, we will generate a standard Gaussian random field so that we have a nice gradient:

```
# Generate a vector field with a gradient
from scipy.ndimage.filters import gaussian_filter
x = np.arange(0,10,0.5)
y = np.arange(0,10,0.5)
phi = gaussian_filter(np.random.uniform(size=(20,20)), sigma=5)
```

```
plt.subplot(141)
plt.imshow(phi, interpolation='none')
plt.title(r'$\Phi$')
plt.subplot(142)
plt.imshow(np.gradient(phi)[0], interpolation='none')
plt.title(r'$\partial_x\Phi$')
plt.subplot(143)
plt.title(r'$\partial_y\Phi$')
plt.imshow(np.gradient(phi)[1], interpolation='none')
plt.subplot(144)
plt.title(r'$\|\nabla \Phi\|$')
plt.imshow(np.linalg.norm(np.gradient(phi), axis=0), interpolation='none')
plt.gcf().set_size_inches(8,4)
```

Following is the output of the preceding code:

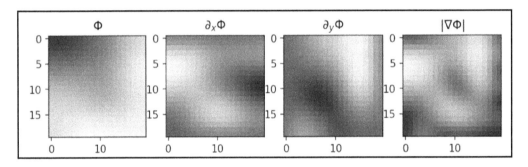

Let's take look at the components of the vector field from the preceding output which shows the Gaussian random fields. The first plot is called **Phi**. The next plot shows the variation in X, and the one after shows the variation in Y. As we can see, the variation in the X direction, the gradient, and the variation in the Y direction are different, as is the magnitude or total amount of variation.

The greatest amount of variation is shown in the X direction, and the most change is shown in the Y direction. We will take a look at how we can plot these two components together.

Since this is a vector, we are actually dealing with four-dimensional data. The following output shows the scalar, three-dimensional data of Phi:

```
# Vectors with quiver
plt.imshow(phi, extent=(0,10,0,10), interpolation='none', origin='lower')
```

We will get the following output:

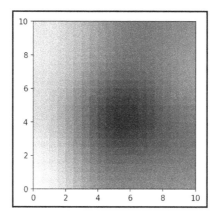

Making vector plots with quiver

We want to plot both the X and the Y changes together. For this, we can use the quiver method. To use the quiver method, insert the (phi) [1] and (phi) [0] gradients into the gradient method. When we call this default set of arguments, the x and y positions, as well as the length of the x and y vectors we provide, will create the following vector field:

```
# Vectors with quiver
plt.imshow(phi, extent=(0,10,0,10), interpolation='none', origin='lower')
plt.quiver(x, y, np.gradient(phi)[0], np.gradient(phi)[1])
```

Following is the output of the preceding code:

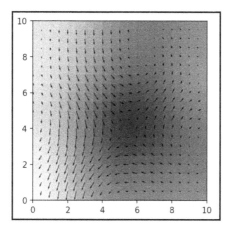

We can also change the scale. Usually, after passing a scale of 1, we would get the same length vectors but, here, the scale isn't a single constant value. Instead, what it says is how many units in the vector dimension are required to give a constant unit length vector, as shown in the following code:

```
# Vector scale
plt.quiver(x, y, np.gradient(phi)[1], np.gradient(phi)[0], scale=1)
```

Following is the output of the preceding code snippet:

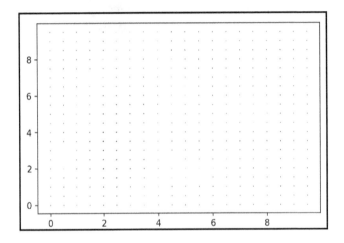

This is why we get bigger vectors with bigger values by changing the `scale` to `10`, as shown in the following output:

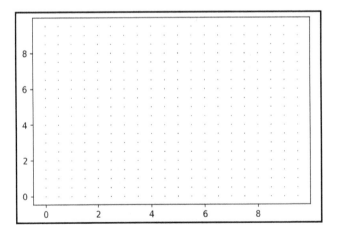

To get bigger vectors with smaller values of scale change the value, that is `scale=0.1`, we can perform the following:

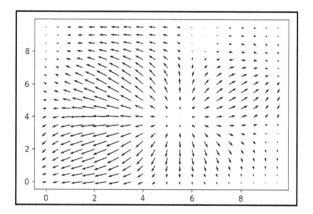

There are a number of different ways for deciding the width, inches, and so on, using the `scale_units` argument. By default, this argument uses `width`. Hence, while specifying `width`, we will get exactly the same output as shown:

```
# Units (x,y,height,width,inches)
plt.quiver(x, y, np.gradient(phi)[1], np.gradient(phi)[0],
scale_units='width', scale=0.1)
```

After, we pass the `inches` function, we get the following:

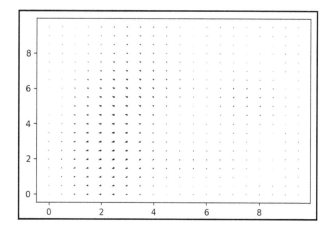

Customizing the appearance of vector plots

This corresponds to what the scale translates into. For instance, a scale unit set to width says that the unit value of 1 is one times the width of your plot. If a scale unit of x says that 1 is one in the width in the x dimension, a scale value of y says the same thing in the y dimension, while the inches says a scale of 1 equals 1 inch long. So, depending on whether or not we want the arrows to scale relative to the size of the image or actual printed image, we would get a value that is independent of the scale of the data itself, which we can specify using the scale units argument.

To customize the appearance of the vector plots, we will take the following steps:

1. The width of the vectors can also be specified, so, in order to have a one percent size, we need to pass a `width` of `0.01`, as shown:

```
# Vector width
plt.quiver(x, y, np.gradient(phi)[1], np.gradient(phi)[0],
width=0.01)
```

By executing the preceding code snippet we will get the following output:

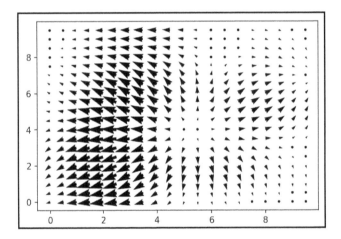

2. We can go even smaller by changing the `width` to `0.001` so that we get nice, thin little arrows:

```
# Vector width
plt.quiver(x, y, np.gradient(phi)[1], np.gradient(phi)[0],
width=0.001)
```

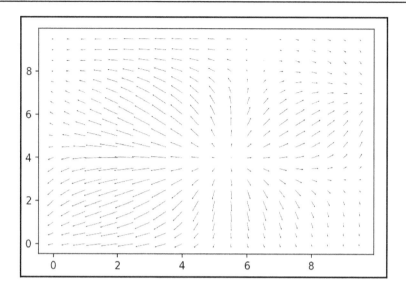

3. We can also pass colors by passing `color='r'`, as follows:

```
# Vector width
plt.quiver(x, y, np.gradient(phi)[1], np.gradient(phi)[0],
color='r')
```

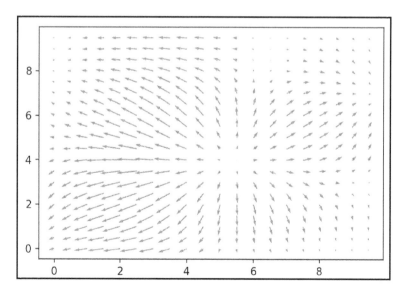

4. Like scatter, we can get individual colors for each of the arrows. By passing the keyword argument `phi`, we can color the vectors as a function, which is a rich way of showing data. Here, we have five-dimensional data, the vector links, and then a color showing the viewer five different kinds of data, not to mention the individual data that varies from point to point. This means that we have a single point conveying five important pieces of information:

```
# Vector Color
plt.quiver(x, y, np.gradient(phi)[1], np.gradient(phi)[0], phi)
```

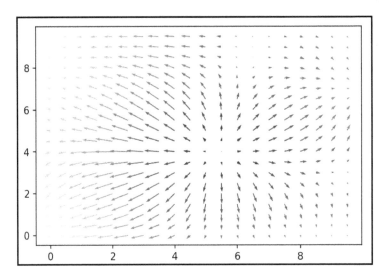

5. We can also change the pivot. The pivot specifies where on the vector X and Y correspond to, so by default we can use `pivot= 'tail'`, and state that the x and y values correspond to the very end. We can use `pivot= 'mid'` and `pivot= 'tip'` as well. The tip, as you might imagine, corresponds to the head part of the vector. As you can see, we have a tail which is the farthest along; we also have the mid in black and the tip in blue. What we are doing is placing these at different positions. Usually, there won't be a reason for you to change this, but if you find that you do need to specify where these x and y coordinates fall on the individual vector arrows, this is the way you can do so:

```
# Pivot (where the vector goes)
plt.quiver(x, y, np.gradient(phi)[1], np.gradient(phi)[0],
color='r', pivot='tail')
plt.quiver(x, y, np.gradient(phi)[1], np.gradient(phi)[0],
color='k', pivot='mid')
plt.quiver(x, y, np.gradient(phi)[1], np.gradient(phi)[0],
color='b', pivot='tip')
```

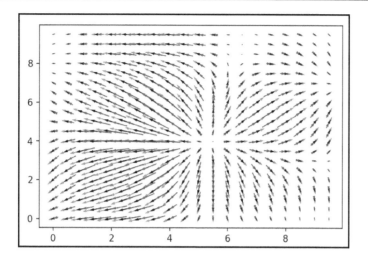

Annotating vector plots with a quiver key

We can also add a key to the vectors by using the `quiverkey` method, and then add the return value that the quiver provides. When we insert the quiver key with the x and y values, say 1 and 9, a string called gradient and another argument saying what the default length will be inserted. We can also add a key to this. By using the quiver key method, we pass the quiver return value, as well as some coordinates in the figure coordinate system (keep in mind this is not the data coordinates), a length that refers to how long in the vector scale we would want this label to be, and a label string called **gradient**. Here, we can see a nice little label:

```
# Key
q = plt.quiver(x, y, np.gradient(phi)[1], np.gradient(phi)[0], color='r')
plt.quiverkey(q, 0.1, 0.9, 0.01, "Gradient")
```

We will get the following output:

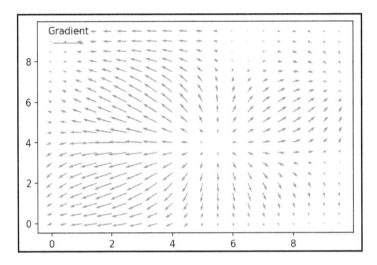

Since the label has the same color as the arrows, we can pass `color = 'k'`, which will show a different colored arrow for the key, which tells us that something that is this long has a vector length of `0.01`. This is a nice way of telling the viewer how these lengths correspond to data values:

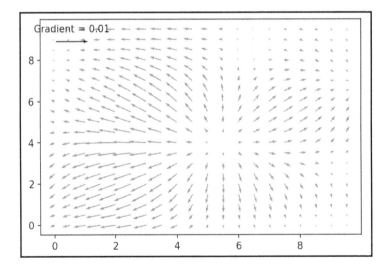

Making stream plots

We also have another option for plotting vectors, and that is by using the `streamplot` as shown in the following points:

1. The stream plot will actually follow stream lines, so they will generate smooth curves that go along the lines. An example of this is shown in the following code:

```
# Stream plot
plt.streamplot(x, y, np.gradient(phi)[1], np.gradient(phi)[0])
```

Following is the output of the preceding code:

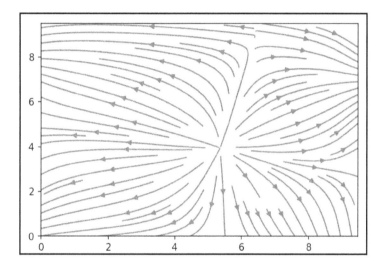

In the stream plot, we can specify a density argument that tells us how many of these lines per unit area we get. We can see that a `density` of 1 gives you more or less what we had before.

2. When we double the `density` with 2, we get a variation, as follows:

```
# Stream plot density
plt.streamplot(x, y, np.gradient(phi)[1], np.gradient(phi)[0],
density=2)
```

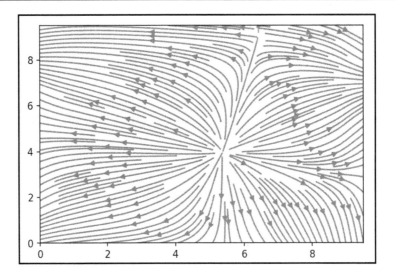

3. When we double the density with `0.5`, we get the following:

```
# Stream plot density
plt.streamplot(x, y, np.gradient(phi)[1], np.gradient(phi)[0],
density=0.5)
```

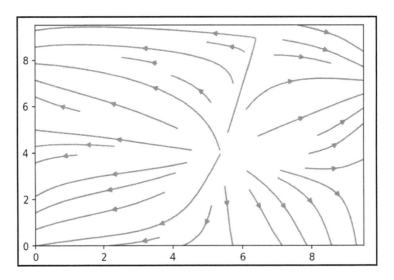

4. Next, we will customize the color argument. Just like with the quiver, we will make individual colors for the lines. Unlike the quivers, which had different arrows for each different point, we can actually change the colors along our line, like so:

```
# Stream plot linewidth
delta = phi-np.mean(phi)
plt.streamplot(x, y, np.gradient(phi)[1], np.gradient(phi)[0],
color=phi)
```

Following is the output of the preceding code:

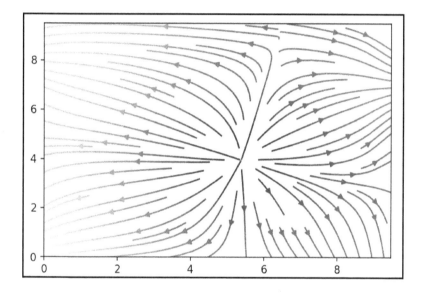

5. To change the width of the lines, we can color them based on the value. The size of these lines can also be changed based on changing `phi`. By doing this, we get infinitesimal lines near the middle of the plot, where the average value is more or less equal to the current value of this scalar field:

```
# Stream plot linewidth
delta = phi-np.mean(phi)
plt.streamplot(x, y, np.gradient(phi)[1], np.gradient(phi)[0],
linewidth=delta)
```

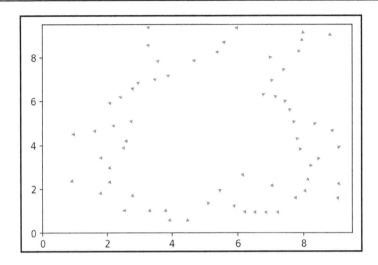

Statistics with boxes and violins

This section describes how to make box plots and outliers within the data and how to customize the appearance of plots.

Making box plots to show the interquartile ranges and the outliers

We will begin by importing the data. Start by generating normal Gaussian distributions with a couple of different properties, as follows:

```
# Generate some Normal distributions with different properties
rands1 = np.random.normal(size=500)
rands2 = np.random.normal(scale=2, size=500)
rands3 = np.random.normal(loc=1, scale=0.5, size=500)
gaussians = (rands1, rands2, rands3)
```

1. Make some box plots out of this data. Hence, by making a box plot of Gaussians, we can comment to suppress the output. Here, we can see that we get the following plot:

```
# Basic Boxplot
plt.boxplot(gaussians);
```

Following is the output of the preceding code:

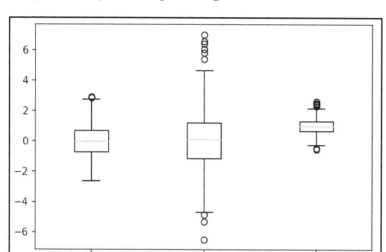

This kind of box plot was invented at Bell Labs about fifty years ago. Each of the boxes shows the interquartile range around the mean of the values; the black edges show the 75th and 25th percentile, and each of the little dots (plus signs), known as **Flyers**, show the outliers within the dataset. From this simple plot, we can automatically see that the first two distributions have the same mean but a different standard deviation and a different interquartile range, while the third box has a different mean and a different interquartile range.

2. We can also add labels if all three boxes aren't very descriptive. We do this by using a tuple of strings. By adding the keywords `first`, `second`, and `third`, we get the following:

```
# Labels
plt.boxplot(gaussians, labels=("first", "second", "third"));
```

We will get the following output:

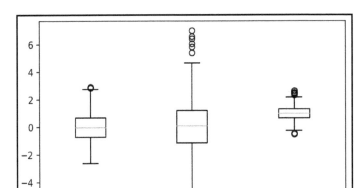

By default, this will usually give you decent width values. This will automatically scale things. However, we can also make them smaller or larger.

3. Making a smaller width can be done as follows:

```
# Box widths
plt.boxplot(gaussians, widths=0.1);
```

Following is the output of the preceding code:

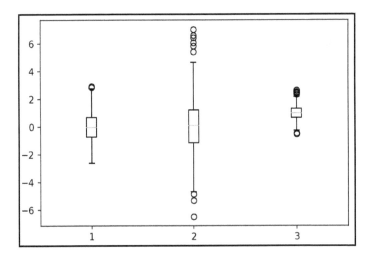

4. Making a larger width can be done as follows by changing the `width` to `0.7`:

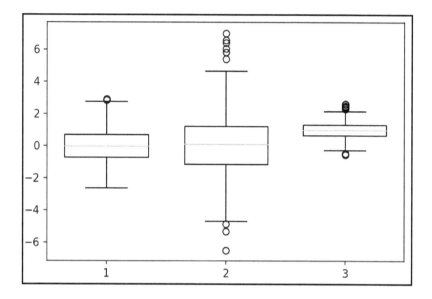

5. We can also choose to pass a tuple for each of these values, depending on what the data will try to show. For example, it could show one thin, one wide, and one very wide boxplot, as shown in the following code:

```
# Box widths
plt.boxplot(gaussians, widths=(0.1,0.5,0.7));
```

The preceding code gives the following output:

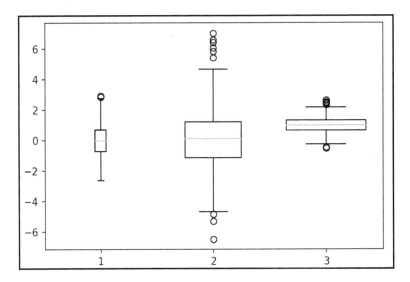

6. We can also set these boxes to be horizontal when we set `vert= 'False'`. We can also get horizontal box plots and customize the appearance of the outliers like so:

```
# Horizontal boxes w/ vert
plt.boxplot(gaussians, vert=False);
```

Following is the output of the preceding code:

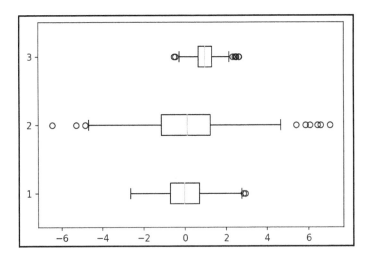

7. To customize the appearance of the outliers, we could use `sym = '.'` and change these outliers to use dots, as follows:

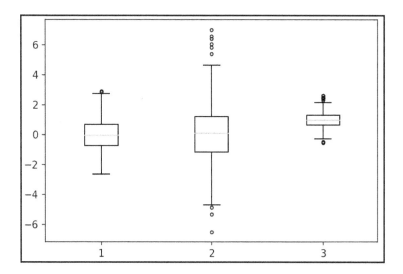

8. We can also use an empty string `sym=''`:

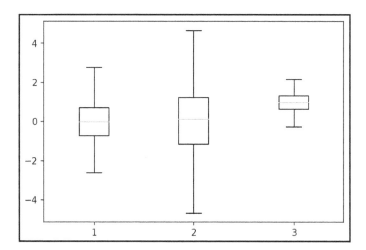

Making violin plots show different distributions

What if we don't want to show the interquartile range of data, but just the full distribution? We have a similar kind of plot called a **violin plot** for this. We will add some extra different kinds of distributions to it that are not Gaussian.

We will include a `lognormal`, which is a Gaussian and logarithmic space. This is often used in astrophysics to describe a wide variety of physical phenomena. We will also include a pareto distribution, which is used frequently in economics since it describes a lot of economic systems.

First, we will take a look at a violin plot:

```
# Some other kinds of distributions
rands4 = np.random.lognormal(size=500, sigma=0.5)
rands5 = np.random.pareto(size=500, a=5)
dists = (rands1, rands4, rands5)
# Basic Violin plot
plt.violinplot(dists);
```

We will get the following output:

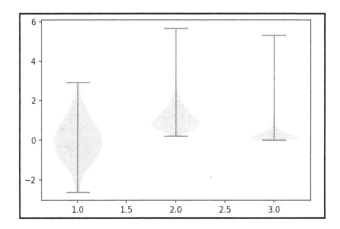

In the preceding output, a lot of information is conveyed.

The different distributions are as follows:

- In the first distribution, we can see that the Gaussian has a little bit of a bump as we are sampling it imperfectly. We have 500 points, so there's a short noise.
- Log normal (the second distribution) is mostly centered on 0 and has a long tail.
- The pareto distribution is incredibly unequal.

Hence, this is a great way of conveying the differences in distributions that we see within multiple datasets.

By adding some extra annotations and setting `showmeans = True`, we get an extra, line which is the mean or average value:

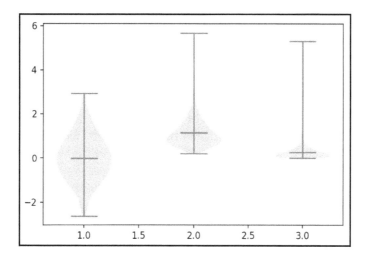

We can also show the median, which is the value at which half the data points lie on each side. The mean is the value that we get by adding all of the values together and then dividing by the number of values there are, whereas the median is the true middle. The output is as follows:

```
# Show Median & Means
plt.violinplot(dists, showmeans=True, showmedians=True);
```

Following is the output of the preceding code:

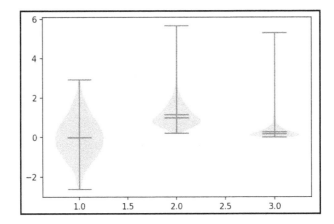

Customizing the appearance of plots

In the preceding output, we can see that all of the lines makes telling the difference between them difficult. To customize the appearance of the violin plots, we must return the value of plot n, and put it into something so that we can look at it. Hence, when we print this `vplot`, we get a dictionary with some keys:

```
# Show Median & Means
vplot = plt.violinplot(dists, showmeans=True, showmedians=True);
print(vplot)
```

We will get the following output:

```
{'bodies': [<matplotlib.collections.PolyCollection object at 0x00000000090B99B0>, <matplotlib.collections.PolyCollection object
at 0x00000000090A0080>, <matplotlib.collections.PolyCollection object at 0x00000000090A0710>], 'cmeans': <matplotlib.collection
s.LineCollection object at 0x00000000090B9860>, 'cmaxes': <matplotlib.collections.LineCollection object at 0x0000000000912C400>,
'cmins': <matplotlib.collections.LineCollection object at 0x0000000000912C940>, 'cbars': <matplotlib.collections.LineCollection
object at 0x0000000000912CFD0>, 'cmedians': <matplotlib.collections.LineCollection object at 0x00000000000910B6A0>}
```

The keys are as follows:

```
dict_keys(['bodies', 'cmeans', 'cmaxes', 'cmins', 'cbars', 'cmedians'])
```

Each of the keys corresponds to the different components of the plot. The `'bodies'` key is a list of objects used for the distributions, while the `'cmedians'`, `'cmaxes'`, `'cBar'`, `'cmeans'`, and `'cmins'` keys are all of the line elements.

We will change the color of the medians so that we can see the difference between medians and the means. Hence, by typing `vplot ['cmedians']`, we can set the color to blue. The following code shows the difference between these medians and the means:

```
# Getting the components
vplot = plt.violinplot(dists, showmedians=True, showmeans=True)
vplot['cmedians'].set_color('b')
```

Following is the output of the preceding code:

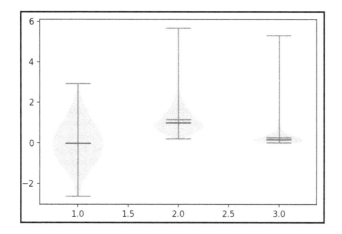

To make the bodies a different color, we need to access each individual distribution. Index the plots like an array so that the first distribution has a black background and the second has a green background. Leave the third as it is:

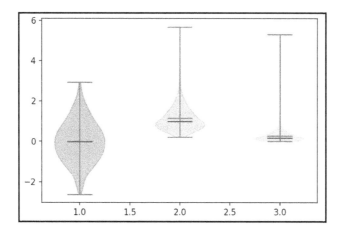

The violin plot requires a different syntax for each of the components. `set_color` takes a list or a tuple of colors. While passing 1, it will simply pass the same value to each of the colors. In terms of the rest of the violin plots, we can use the same kinds of arguments that we passed to the box plot to flip them, label them, and so on.

In the next section, we're going to take a look at how to visualize ordinal and tabular data, where one of your axes isn't really a number.

Visualizing ordinal and tabular data

In this section, we will talk about tabular and ordinal data, where we don't have an x axis and y axis. We're going to take a look at the following topics:

- Pie charts
- Tables
- How to customize the appearance of plots

Pie charts

Let's take a look at the fractions of gases that exist in our atmosphere. The following content shows the code and output for Nitrogen, which is 78 percent of our atmosphere, Oxygen, which is 21 percent, and Argon, which is 1 percent. Now, naturally, Nitrogen, Oxygen, and Argon are not exactly numerical values. Hence, we cannot really plot these things against each other in the standard way. This is where we can use a pie chart as a best practice to display these differences:

1. First, we must set the aspect ratio to equal here. This gives a standard pie chart, as follows:

```
# Basic Pie Chart
fracs = (78, 21, 1)
labels = ('Nitrogen', 'Oxygen', 'Argon')
plt.pie(fracs, labels=labels);
plt.gca().set_aspect('equal')
```

We will get the following output:

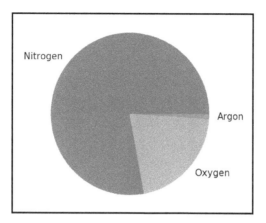

2. To customize the preceding pie chart, we can highlight the **Oxygen** part. We will add another tuple and call it `explode` argument. These tuple values can be used to pull slices out. Here, we can see that **Oxygen** was sliced out by 20 percent:

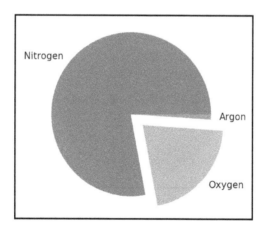

3. The colors can also be changed in the same way by passing a tuple with the same length as the number of slices, as shown in the following code:

```
# colors
fracs = (78, 21, 1)
labels = ('Nitrogen', 'Oxygen', 'Argon')
plt.pie(fracs, colors=('k', 'c', 'g'), labels=labels);
plt.gca().set_aspect('equal')
```

We will get the following output:

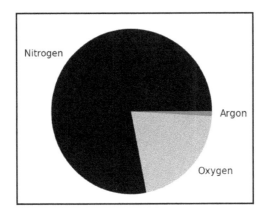

4. We can also add a shadow by setting the `shadow` keyword argument to `True`. By doing this, you get a nice little shadow:

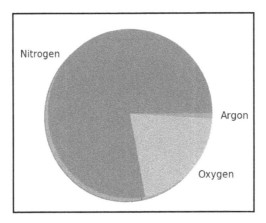

5. To change the radius of the pie chart so that it's 50 percent smaller, that is `radius=0.5`, we can use the following code:

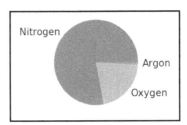

6. To show the percentages of the chart, we can insert `autopct= "%2.0f %%"`. This will display the percentage values as well. This can either be a format string or a function that returns a string:

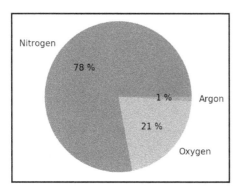

7. We can also set `pctdistance` with what fraction or radius of the pie chart these labels get applied at. To have them near the edge, we can set this to 90 percent; that is `0.9`:

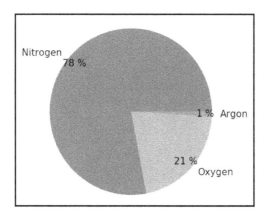

8. To have the labels near the radius, set it to 50 percent; that is `0.5`:

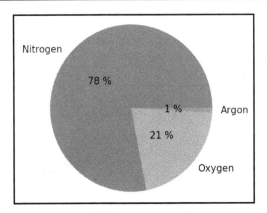

By setting the `pctdistance` to 0.1, we get the labels 78 percent, 21 percent, and 1 percent much closer to the radius.

Tables

To display the numerical values 78, 21, and 1, we will use the table method that Matplotlib provides and give the keyword argument cell data or cell text.

By inserting `colLabels` and `rowLabels`, we get a nice labeled table:

```
# Add a table
fracs = (78, 21, 1)
labels = ('Nitrogen', 'Oxygen', 'Argon')
plt.pie(fracs, labels=labels)
plt.table(cellText=[fracs], colLabels=labels, rowLabels=["fraction"])
plt.gca().set_aspect('equal')
```

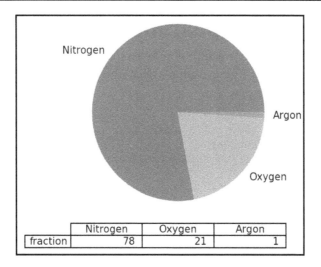

This is a nice way to supplement data. If we have a plot where we have a couple of numbers to show alongside it, the plot table is the way to do this. You may recall that pandas provides a way to automatically do this.

We can also change the location of this table. We will change the location of the table so that it's to the left, as shown in the following code:

```
# Change location w/ loc
fracs = (78, 21, 1)
labels = ('Nitrogen', 'Oxygen', 'Argon')
plt.pie(fracs, labels=labels)
plt.table(cellText=[fracs], rowLabels=['Fraction'], colLabels=labels,
loc='left')
plt.gca().set_aspect('equal')
```

We will get the following output:

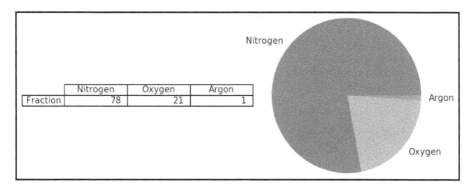

Customizing the appearance of plots

To change the appearance of the preceding table so that Nitrogen is blue, Oxygen is green, and Argon is red, we will pass some arguments in the following code:

```
# Cell colours w/ rowColours, cellColours & colColours
fracs = (78, 21, 1)
labels = ('Nitrogen', 'Oxygen', 'Argon')
plt.pie(fracs, labels=labels)
plt.table(cellText=[fracs], rowLabels=['Fraction'], colLabels=labels,
colColours=['b','g','r'])
plt.gca().set_aspect('equal')
```

The column labels will change. The output is as follows:

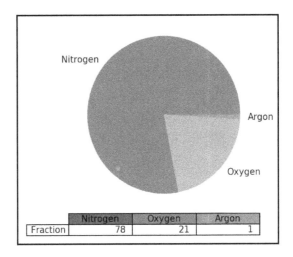

To change the color of the Fraction row, change callColors to cellColors. Since it has to match the same dimensions, we can give the same dimensions a three by one matrix. By doing this, we get colored cells:

```
# Cell colours w/ rowColours, cellColours & colColours
fracs = (78, 21, 1)
labels = ('Nitrogen', 'Oxygen', 'Argon')
plt.pie(fracs, labels=labels)
plt.table(cellText=[fracs], rowLabels=['Fraction'], colLabels=labels,
cellColours=[['b','g','r']])
plt.gca().set_aspect('equal')
```

The output for the preceding code is as follows:

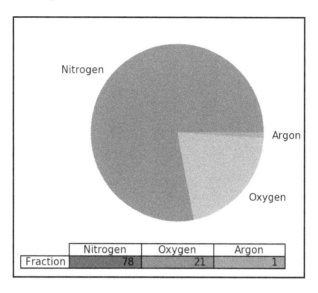

Summary

In this chapter, we learned how to plot on non-Cartesian axes and how to plot high-dimensional vector field data. We also studied how to plot different kinds of statistical distributions with box and violin plots. Finally, we learned how to display small numbers of ordinal and tabular data with pie charts and tables.

In the next chapter, we will look at how to plot 3D and geospatial data.

3D and Geospatial Plots

4

From the previous chapter, we learned about how to plot on non-Cartesian axes and how to plot high dimensional vector field data. This chapter explains how to add 3D axes and plotting on the 3D axes. The significance of this chapter is the basemap method, where we choose between different kinds of map projections.

In this chapter, we will learn about the following:

- How to set up and manipulate 3D axes
- The different kinds of 3D plots that Matplotlib provides
- How to use the basemap class to generate geospatial plots
- How to apply these plots on map projections
- How to add geography to the plots

Plotting with 3D axes

We will begin by importing `numpy`, `matplotlib`, and `pyplot`, as shown here:

```
import numpy as np
import matplotlib as mpl
import matplotlib.pyplot as plt
%matplotlib notebook
# Set up figure size and DPI for screen demo
plt.rcParams['figure.figsize'] = (6,4)
plt.rcParams['figure.dpi'] = 150
```

How to add 3D axes to a figure

We will use the Matplotlib inline magic in Jupyter Notebook to create our plotting setup. Begin by making a new figure and add some axes to this figure. Add a subplot, as shown in the following code, along with the `projection= '3D'` keyword argument:

```
# Make a Axes3D
from mpl_toolkits.mplot3d import Axes3D
fig = plt.figure()
ax = fig.add_subplot(111, projection='3d')
```

We see that the axes generated are indeed 3D, with an orthogonal projection shown in the following output:

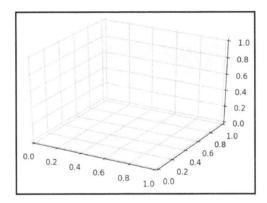

How to use the interactive backend to manipulate the 3D plots

In order to get the full 3D effect of our plot, we will **Restart** the kernel before using this plot, to allow us to bring in a different backend for Matplotlib. We will import this as usual, but replace `matplotlib` with `matplotlib notebook`, as shown here:

```
%matplotlib notebook
# Set up figure size and DPI for screen demo
plt.rcParams['figure.figsize'] = (6,4)
plt.rcParams['figure.dpi'] = 150
```

From the output of the preceding code, we get a different backend. So, rather than generating a static image, we can save a PNG image (the output), with which we will use a bit of JavaScript to generate an interactive plot. There are also some widgets present on the left-hand side of the plot, as shown:

When we click and drag the output, it actually manipulates where the camera is looking within the plot. We can also go back to the previous view, reverse these changes, or revert to the original view as shown in the preceding image.

Finally, we select one of these widgets that change the limits of the axes, and download the output in PNG format. In order to place the image in a fixed format, hit the **Stop** button shown at the top right to stop interaction, which will create a fixed image which we can now download.

How to plot on the 3D axes

To insert something on the plot we've created, make the new axes and generate 500 random points with random *x*, *y*, and *z* positions:

```
# Add a 3D Scatterplot
x = np.random.normal(size=500)
y = np.random.normal(size=500)
z = np.random.normal(size=500)
fig = plt.figure()
ax = fig.add_subplot(111, projection='3d')
ax.scatter(x,y,z)
```

When we call `scatter` on this axis object, we get a 3D projected scatter plot, as shown here:

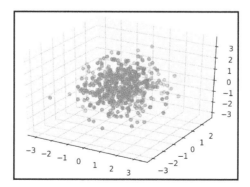

As we hover over this 3D scatter plot, we get a 3D Gaussian (essentially a ball of points). A 3D Gaussian approximates a lot of interesting phenomena; for example, it's a reasonable approximation of certain kinds of star clusters in astrophysics.

We will color these balls of points as we did with our standard scatter. This scatter actually behaves like the standard 2D version. So, let's first take the norm of x, y, and z, as shown in the following code:

```
# Add a 3D Scatterplot
x = np.random.normal(size=500)
y = np.random.normal(size=500)
z = np.random.normal(size=500)
fig = plt.figure()
ax = fig.add_subplot(111, projection='3d')
ax.scatter(x,y,z,c=np.linalg.norm([x,y,z], axis=0))
```

We get the output as shown in the following plot—a nicely colored bundle of points, with the hue of each one based on its distance from the origin, as shown here:

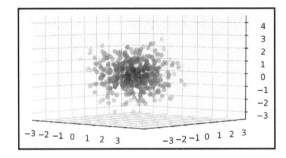

Hence, we see here that it is quite easy to generate 3D plots in Matplotlib. In the past, generating 3D plots required jumping through a lot of hoops, and often it was easier to use other tools, but the 3D plotting infrastructure within Matplotlib has actually matured quite a bit in the past few years.

Looking at various 3D plot types

This section describes how to add line and scatter plots and how to add 3D contour types.

How to rotate the camera in 3D plots

We have a parametric spiral curve that ascends along the different axes which is described in the following points:

1. We have spiral curve along the z axis, as shown in the following code:

    ```
    # Line plot
    fig = plt.figure()
    ax = fig.add_subplot(111, projection='3d')
    theta = np.linspace(-4 * np.pi, 4 * np.pi, 100)
    z = np.linspace(-2, 2, 100)
    r = z**2 + 1
    x = r * np.sin(theta)
    y = r * np.cos(theta)
    ax.plot(x,y,z)
    ```

    Hence, here we see our spiral in the 3D plot:

    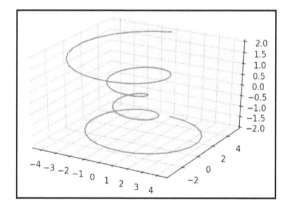

2. If we take a look at the `view_init` method, we have two keyword arguments: elevation, which is given by `elev`, and azimuth, which is given by `azim`. These are measured in angles in degrees; the former describes the elevation of the plane, and the latter, the azimuth, describes the rotation:

    ```
    # Rotating camera angles: elevation & azimuth
    fig = plt.figure()
    ax = fig.add_subplot(111, projection='3d')
    theta = np.linspace(-4 * np.pi, 4 * np.pi, 100)
    z = np.linspace(-2, 2, 100)
    r = z**2 + 1
    x = r * np.sin(theta)
    y = r * np.cos(theta)
    ```

```
ax.plot(x,y,z)
ax.view_init(elev=0)
```

Hence, if we set the elevation to 0, our perspective shifts to look at this side, as shown here:

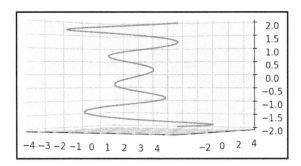

3. When we set the elevation to 90, we look from the top, as shown here:

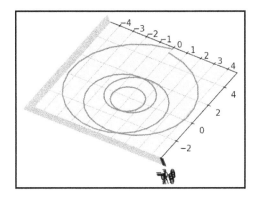

We can also rotate all the way through a full 360 degrees, as well.

4. For the azimuth, we are looking at various rotations:

```
# Rotating camera angles: elevation & azimuth
fig = plt.figure()
ax = fig.add_subplot(111, projection='3d')
theta = np.linspace(-4 * np.pi, 4 * np.pi, 100)
z = np.linspace(-2, 2, 100)
r = z**2 + 1
x = r * np.sin(theta)
y = r * np.cos(theta)
ax.plot(x,y,z)
ax.view_init(azim=0)
```

So, an azimuth of 0 looks straight on at one of our axes, as shown here:

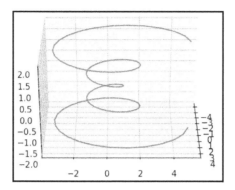

5. In order to look at the *y* axis, we can set `azim` to `90`, which gives the following output:

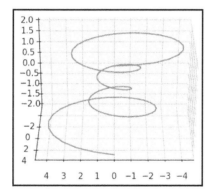

6. Likewise, when we set this to `180`, we get the following perspective:

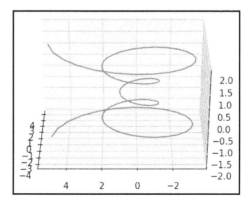

Hence, this is how we can rotate through the full 360 degree angle range for both the azimuth and the elevation to get the perspective we want.

How to add line and scatter plots

To generate a more complicated plot, generate a three-dimensional potential. This is called a **Goldstone potential**, which is an important energy potential in physics used to describe a lot of things, including the Higgs mechanism. We will look at the scatter plot of this Goldstone potential, as shown in the following snippet:

```
# Scatter plot
fig = plt.figure()
ax = fig.add_subplot(111, projection='3d')
x,y = np.meshgrid(np.arange(-10,10,0.5), np.arange(-10,10,0.5))
r = np.linalg.norm([x,y], axis=0)
goldstone = -160*np.power(r,2)+np.power(r,4)
ax.scatter(x,y,goldstone)
```

1. Here, we see a nice scatter plot:

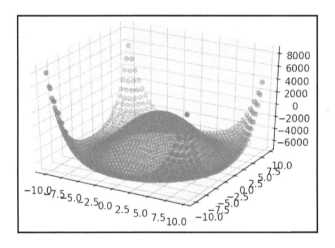

2. Also, we can pass all of the same kind of arguments here that we could pass for a two-dimensional scatter plot. We can change the colors, as shown in the following snippet:

```
# Scatter plot
fig = plt.figure()
ax = fig.add_subplot(111, projection='3d')
x,y = np.meshgrid(np.arange(-10,10,0.5), np.arange(-10,10,0.5))
r = np.linalg.norm([x,y], axis=0)
```

```
goldstone = -160*np.power(r,2)+np.power(r,4)
ax.scatter(x,y,goldstone, c='r')
```

The output of this is as follows:

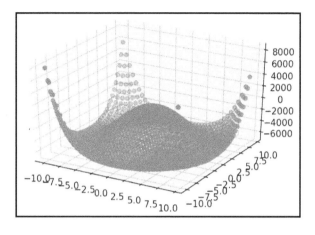

3. We can also change the sizes of the standard scatter plot keyword arguments that we get with a 2D plot. We can do this in 3D as well, by adding `s=1`:

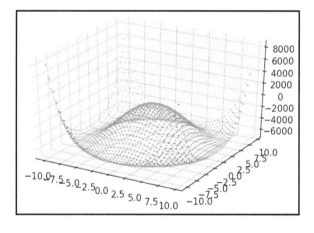

How to add wireframe, surface, and triangular surface plots

By considering the plot not just as a bunch of points, but as something filled in, we can use either the `wireframe` keyword or the `wireframe` method on the new axes, as shown here:

```
# Wireframe plot: r/c, stride & count
fig = plt.figure()
ax = fig.add_subplot(111, projection='3d')
x,y = np.meshgrid(np.arange(-10,10,0.5), np.arange(-10,10,0.5))
r = np.linalg.norm([x,y], axis=0)
goldstone = -160*np.power(r,2)+np.power(r,4)
ax.plot_wireframe(x,y,goldstone)
```

1. In the preceding snippet, we pass `x`, `y` and `goldstone`, which gives us a nice surface, as shown here:

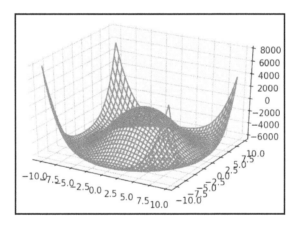

2. In order to change how Matplotlib decides where to put this wireframe, there are two options: we have `stride` and `count`. This includes both the row stride and the column stride. By default, it is set to `1`. We will double that, as shown in the following code:

```
# Wireframe plot: r/c, stride & count
fig = plt.figure()
ax = fig.add_subplot(111, projection='3d')
x,y = np.meshgrid(np.arange(-10,10,0.5), np.arange(-10,10,0.5))
r = np.linalg.norm([x,y], axis=0)
goldstone = -160*np.power(r,2)+np.power(r,4)
ax.plot_wireframe(x,y,goldstone, rstride=4)
```

We can see that the code generates fewer of these lines in the wireframe, basically jumping to every second point, as shown here:

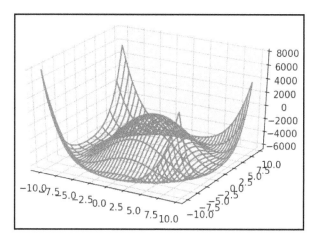

We can also see a different output by changing `rstride` to `10`.

The same can be applied to the columns as well. Hence, when we change from `rstride` to `cstride`, we change the total number of lines.

3. In order to fill the curve in, we use the surface plot method, so that, rather than actually plotting the wireframe, we plot the surface, which also takes these stride arguments. But, by default, the stride is not `1`, but actually `10`; hence, to get the same kind of resolution as before, we have to manually set the strides down to `1`, as shown here:

```
# Surface plot
fig = plt.figure()
ax = fig.add_subplot(111, projection='3d')
x,y = np.meshgrid(np.arange(-10,10,0.5), np.arange(-10,10,0.5))
r = np.linalg.norm([x,y], axis=0)
goldstone = -160*np.power(r,2)+np.power(r,4)
ax.plot_surface(x,y,goldstone, rstride=1, cstride=1)
```

The output of the preceding code is as follows:

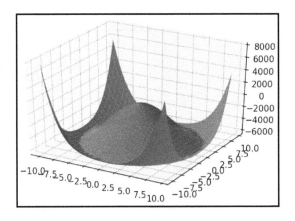

4. To pass a color map argument for a colored surface plot, pass a color which will simply change the color of the surface. We will pass in `cmap='viridis'` and get the same resolution as before, as shown in the following output:

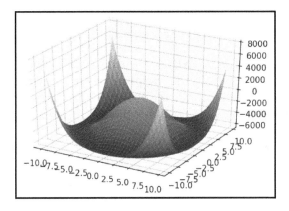

So, this is a nice way of getting visually rich plots that show a lot of information in 3D.

5. Next, to get the connections in our 3D plot to be made based on nearest neighbors, rather than by the array order, we use the tri-surface plot:

```
# Tri-surface plot
fig = plt.figure()
ax = fig.add_subplot(111, projection='3d')
x,y = np.meshgrid(np.arange(-10,10,0.5), np.arange(-10,10,0.5))
r = np.linalg.norm([x,y], axis=0)
```

```
goldstone = -100*np.power(r,2)+np.power(r,4)
x = x[r<10]
y = y[r<10]
goldstone = goldstone[r<10]
ax.plot_trisurf(x,y,goldstone)
```

6. Here, we generate a filled-in surface, where triangles are created based on neighbor nearness, as shown here:

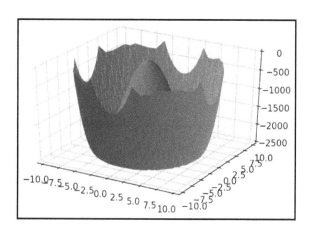

How to add 3D contour types

We also have the ability to add contours to a 3D plot. Try the following code:

```
# Contour plot (filled/unfilled)
fig = plt.figure()
ax = fig.add_subplot(111, projection='3d')
x,y = np.meshgrid(np.arange(-10,10,0.5), np.arange(-10,10,0.5))
r = np.linalg.norm([x,y], axis=0)
goldstone = -200*np.power(r,2)+np.power(r,4)
ax.contour(x,y,goldstone)
```

From this code, we get a nice set of contours in 3D, as shown here:

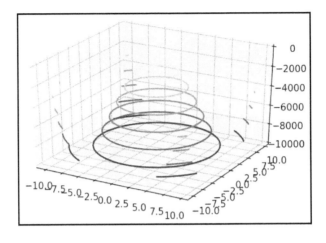

By adding the letter f ahead of `contour`, we get 3D filled contours, as shown here:

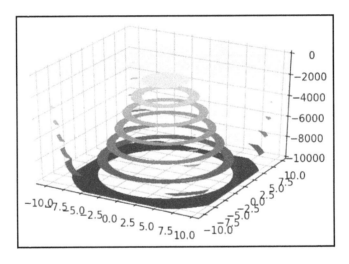

Hence, we see that, in general, most of these methods are very similar to the 2D version of our plot, but with a few extra keyword arguments on top. `contour` has a couple of really neat keyword arguments that are particularly useful, as well.

So, from the preceding output, we see that the code generates contours in the z direction; in other words, it is finding values of equal z height:

1. In order to find values of x, we pass the `zdir` keyword argument:

```
# Contour plot: zdir, offset
fig = plt.figure()
ax = fig.add_subplot(111, projection='3d')
x,y = np.meshgrid(np.arange(-10,10,0.5), np.arange(-10,10,0.5))
r = np.linalg.norm([x,y], axis=0)
goldstone = -200*np.power(r,2)+np.power(r,4)
ax.contour(x,y,goldstone, zdir='x')
```

The following output shows the resulting plot of the contours in the *x* dimension:

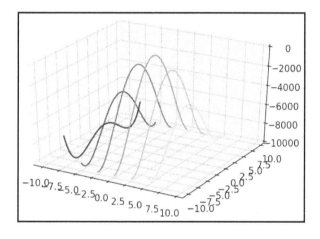

2. Similarly, if we change the value of `zdir` to y, we will get the following:

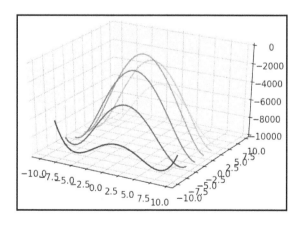

3. By passing an extra keyword argument called offset, we gain the ability to collapse this contour into one dimension. Hence, it turns a 3D plot into a 2D plot, and places it as a slice in the cube that you have in this volume. By setting offset to 10, it projects those contours onto the wall of the plot as shown:

```
# Contour plot: zdir, offset
fig = plt.figure()
ax = fig.add_subplot(111, projection='3d')
x,y = np.meshgrid(np.arange(-10,10,0.5), np.arange(-10,10,0.5))
r = np.linalg.norm([x,y], axis=0)
goldstone = -200*np.power(r,2)+np.power(r,4)
ax.contour(x,y,goldstone, zdir='y', offset=10)
ax.contour(x,y,goldstone, zdir='x', offset=-10)
```

The output looks as follows:

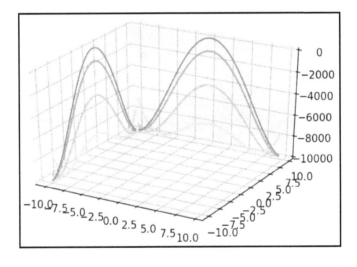

4. However, we notice that the ground surface at the bottom of the cube is empty. So, by setting zdir= 'z', and giving an offset of −10000 (which is where this ground surface is), we see all of the contours projected down, as shown in the following output:

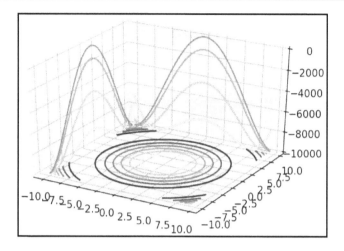

5. To place the 3D plot within the volume, we combine 2D and 3D to get a rich representation of multi-dimensional data using the following code:

```
ax.contour(x,y,goldstone, zdir='z', offset=-10000)
ax.scatter(x,y,goldstone, c=goldstone, cmap='inferno')
```

Hence, here we have a quite remarkably rich combination of data. We have the color and then the projection of the contours onto three walls of this cube, as shown here:

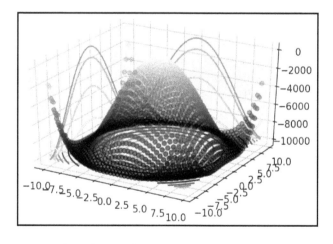

So, with the 3D axis, we can build incredibly rich visualizations out of high dimensional data sets.

The basemap methods

Before we get started, let's think a little bit about map projections. We have already seen the visualized data showing population density in the United States:

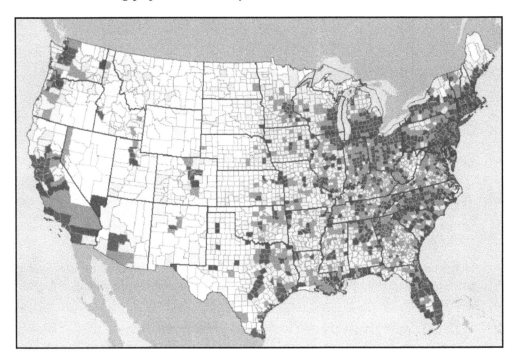

It is known that the earth is a sphere, but your screen is not a sphere, it's actually a flat Euclidean plane. So, translating points from the surface of a sphere onto the points on the surface of this flat plane is actually non-trivial. We can't unroll a sphere into a flat plane without tearing or distorting that sphere, and so, most of the time when you're dealing with a map, you're actually looking at a projection.

But Mercator is only one of many projections. There are other alternative projections, and even projections that don't necessarily end up giving you square edges for your globe, as shown here:

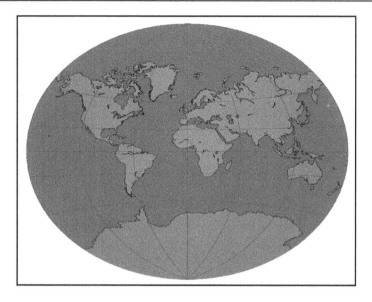

One of the key things when setting up a map is choosing which projection to use. The choice depends on the kind of data you're dealing with: whether or not you're dealing with data across the whole globe, data that is restricted to one region in the Northern or Southern hemisphere, or other particular features of that data. Some map projections will be better than others, and, most importantly, there is a big difference between projections that preserve shape and projections that preserve area.

How to create map projections

Import all of the usual things, as done in the earlier sections. Import `Basemap` from `mpl`, as shown here:

```
from mpl_toolkits.basemap import Basemap
```

 `Basemap` does not come with Matplotlib by default, so we need to do a `pip` install of `basemap`, or, if you're using Anaconda, install it using the inbuilt toolkit.

The simplest map projection we get is the one where we translate latitude and longitude into x and y coordinates, and also when we create a `basemap` object with no projection keyword argument. Each of the following arguments represents a different parameter: `llcrnrlat` shows the minimum latitude, `urcrnrlat` shows the maximum latitude, `llcrnrlon` shows the minimum longitude, `urcrnrlon` shows the maximum longitude, and `lat_ts` shows where to center the map:

```
# Creating the most basic projection
m = Basemap (llcrnrlat=-80, urcrnrlat=80, llcrnrlon=-180,
            urcrnrlon=180, lat_ts=0)
setup_map (m)
plt.show ()
```

The preceding arguments explain the limits and center of the map. We will take a look at the `setup_map` method, as shown in the following code:

```
def setup_map (m):
    m.drawcoastlines ()
    m.fillcontinents (color='coral',lake_color='aqua')
    # draw parallels and meridians.
    m.drawparallels (np.arange (-90.,120.,30.))
    m.drawmeridians (np.arange (0.,420.,60.))
    m.drawmapboundary (fill_color='aqua')
    for y in np.linspace (m.ymax/22,19*m.ymax/22,9):
        for x in np.linspace (m.xmax/22,19*m.xmax/22,12):
            lon, lat = m (x,y,inverse=True)
            m.tissot (lon+5,lat+5,1.5,100,facecolor='k',zorder=10,alpha=0.5)
```

As seen in the preceding snippet, there are two methods to draw parallels and meridians, which are the latitude and longitude lines. We also see the `tissot` method from the output. Tissots are little circles drawn on the map to show how well that map projection distorts or doesn't distort these circles. In a perfectly accurate projection, all of the circles would be the same regular size. The following output shows our basic map projection:

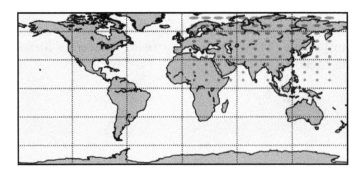

In the preceding output, we see that the circles, even though they should be circular and equal to each other in area, increase in size as they go north, and the shapes get deformed. They become more elliptical. This means that the preceding map is not conformal, which means it doesn't preserve shape and angle; nor is it equal in area.

Consider the following formal map:

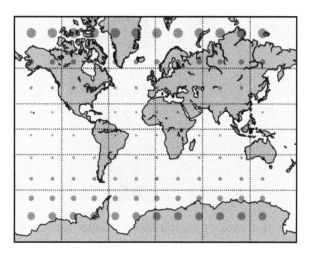

The preceding output shows a map that preserves the accurate shape of the landmasses. The circles stay circular, but don't stay the same size. This is the so-called **Mercator projection**. One of its biggest features is the increase in the area towards the poles.

With the following code, we extend the minimum and maximum latitude all the way up to 89:

```
# Mercator projection
m = Basemap(projection='merc', llcrnrlat=-89, urcrnrlat=89,
            llcrnrlon=-180, urcrnrlon=180,lat_ts=0)
setup_map(m)
plt.show()
```

We can see how the circle metrics close to the poles become arbitrarily large, as shown here:

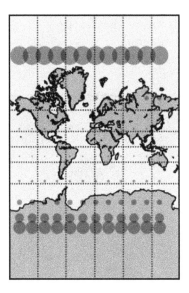

One of the things that the Mercator projection does, due to not being an equal area map, is exaggerate the sizes of features near the poles. A Mercator projection map makes countries like Antarctica and Greenland seems massive, when, in reality, they don't actually cover much area at all. Equally, North America seems to cover far more area than Africa, but in reality, the United States would comfortably fit within Africa, leaving around two thirds of the area of Africa still empty.

Hence, while dealing with presenting data where surface areas are important, Mercator is a poor choice. If, however, shape or angle is all that you care about, then Mercator is perfectly adequate.

How to choose between different kinds of map projections

We will now take a look at an equal area projection, as follows:

```
# Equal Area Projection
m = Basemap(projection='hammer',lon_0=0)
setup_map(m)
plt.show()
```

The following map projection will not distort the sizes of objects, but may distort the shapes of them. This is the so-called **hammer projection**. This is no longer a square grid, but the area of the circles is the same regardless of latitude; their shape, however, is not. We see here that some of them have become elliptical. There are some map projections that do a decent job, but it's not metrically possible to get perfectly conformal and perfectly equal area mount projection.

In this hammer projection, we see that, compared to the Mercator projection, the country of Greenland is tiny compared to the blown-up size it had before. Antarctica, instead of spanning almost a quarter of the map, is relegated to a small island in the South, as it actually is on the surface of the globe:

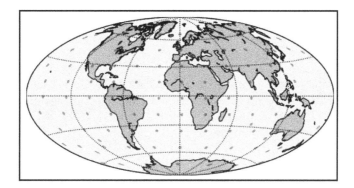

If we do not want to plot the whole surface of the earth but just focus on a region, we can use maps to plot a small region. Hence, here, we use a conformal projection called `lcc` with a width of 5×10^6 meters.

The `width` and `height` keyword arguments are given in meters. Let's take a look at the region covering latitude 1 to latitude 2 and centered on longitude 0. So, 0 is a center and `lat_1` and `lat_2` are the edges:

```
# Just plotting a region
m = Basemap(width=5e6,height=4e6,projection='lcc',
            lat_1=45.,lat_2=55,lat_0=49.5,lon_0=8.7, resolution='l')
m.drawcoastlines()
m.fillcontinents(color='coral',lake_color='aqua')
# draw parallels and meridians.
m.drawparallels(np.arange(-90.,120.,30.))
m.drawmeridians(np.arange(0.,420.,60.))
m.drawmapboundary(fill_color='aqua')
plt.show()
```

When we run the preceding code, we get the following plot of Europe:

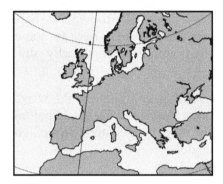

There are about 24 different kinds of projections available in basemap, but the ones that we've discussed so far are the most important.

We will look at one more kind of projection. These are projections that give you a perspective of the Earth that you would get from space. The simplest one is the orthographic projection, as shown here:

```
# Orthographic projection
m = Basemap(projection='ortho',lon_0=10,lat_0=20)
setup_map(m)
plt.show()
```

The output of the preceding code is as follows:

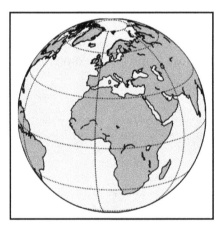

The preceding diagram shows a view of the globe that we would get from an arbitrarily distant observer, so there's none of the distortion that you get from being close to the surface. We see that Tissot is perfect on this projection, as we are dealing with an actual sphere of projection, and not trying to unroll the surface of this sphere. This is the only kind of projection that actually preserves both area and shape, as we are no longer trying to convolve the Earth's spherical surface onto some sort of flat plane.

We can also take the `geos` projection, which is the view that a geostationary satellite would get, as follows:

```
# Geostationary projection
m = Basemap(projection='geos',lon_0=-79.5)
setup_map(m)
plt.show()
```

Hence, preceding the equator at moderate distance there is a projection effect, but if we really want to take a look from an arbitrary distance above the Earth's surface, there is the nearsighted projection, called the `nsper` projection, as shown here:

```
# Near-Sided perspective projection
m = Basemap(projection='nsper',lon_0=-114, lat_0=51, satellite_height=4e8)
setup_map(m)
plt.show()
```

When we run the preceding code, we see that our view is centered on Calgary in Canada. We have placed the satellite at a height of 400,000 kilometers, which is the distance to the Moon:

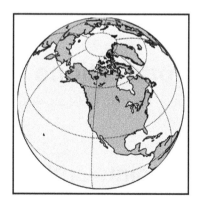

We would see the distance of the moon right above Calgary. As this is a projection that has perspective, we can zoom in. So, we see how the globe would look when the `satellite_height= '4e7'`.

We can also get a higher resolution image by inserting `resolution= '1'` into our projection code, allowing us to take a look at what the Earth's surface would look like from the **International Space Station** (**ISS**). We can also see, at this height, that we don't actually get to see the entire surface of the Earth, as seen in the following output:

```
# Near-Sided perspective projection
m = Basemap(projection='nsper',lon_0=-114, lat_0=51,
            satellite_height=4e5, resolution='1')
setup_map(m)
plt.show()
```

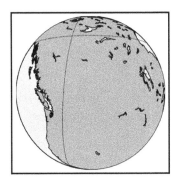

Further reading

For further reference, we can take a look at the basemap documentation, available at `https://matplotlib.org/basemap/`.

Plotting on map projections

This section describes how to plot on the map projections and how to draw a day/night terminator.

How to add simple points and lines to our plots

We can see, from the preceding map, that we have Europe in the middle. We will plot some data points and some curves with lines all over Europe. We will begin by putting down a cross or a point. So the latitude and longitude of Heidelberg is `8.7` degrees east and `49.5` degrees north.

We will start with the scatter method. So the scatter behaves just like we are used to it behaving from the standard Cartesian Euclidean projections. Input the code as follows:

```
# Projecting with and without latlon
m = Basemap(width=1.2e7,height=9e6,projection='lcc',
            lat_1=.45,lat_2=.55,lat_0=49.5,lon_0=8.7)
setup_map(m)
HD = (8.7, 49.5)
plt.show()
```

We will get the output as shown:

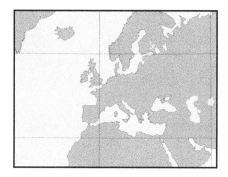

There is actually another way of plotting the cross or a point without having to use the map projection explicitly to convert these coordinates. Hence, when we add an extra keyword argument called `latlon`, and set that to `True`, it will automatically pass these x and y coordinates through the map projection to convert them into map coordinates, as shown in the following output:

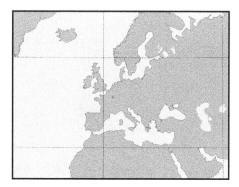

So either way, this works perfectly well for converting coordinates from one coordinate system to the other. There is not much difference between the two. We have seen a single point here, but we can also plot multiple points.

To plot a line right across Europe connecting two points, the following diagram shows a nice little black line going from just above Spain all the way into the edge of Europe:

When we add more than two points, the straight line shown in the previous output gets a curve.

The reason that the line changes into a curve is that we are giving a range of longitude coordinates, but just a single latitude coordinate, so having more than one point with the same latitude coordinate will actually draw an arc of equal latitude.

How to draw great circles

Next, we will take a look at the great circle method. Here, we can actually draw great circles that explicitly connect two points using the shortest distance. We will draw a horizontal and vertical lines between different points:

```
# The shortest distance: the great circle
m = Basemap(width=1.2e7,height=9e6,projection='lcc',
lat_1=45.,lat_2=55,lat_0=49.5,lon_0=8.7)
setup_map(m)
m.drawgreatcircle(-10,45,60,45, color='g', lw=3, linestyle='--')
m.drawgreatcircle(0,50,10,0, color='b', lw=3, linestyle='--')
m.plot(np.linspace(-10,60,20), 45*np.ones(20), 'g-', latlon=True, lw=3)
m.plot(np.linspace(0,10,20), np.linspace(50,0,20), 'b-', latlon=True, lw=3)
plt.show()
```

Here, we see the great circle connection between two points is the dashed curve, which has an equal latitude and arbitrary line between two points in the solid curve.

Oftentimes, when you're trying to draw structures, you are not actually dealing with real data that you have pulled in, and, instead, you want to draw things like boundaries, regions, and connecting points between areas. Say, for example, that you're trying to plot flight data—be very careful as to what is actually going on there, as what appears to be a straight line on the surface of a map may not actually be the shortest distance between two curves. The particular projection that is used makes great circles has straight lines, but different projections will not necessarily do that.

When we perform a cylindrical projection, we see that what was previously a great circle route becomes a curved route, as shown here:

```
# The shortest distance: the great circle
m = Basemap(width=1.2e7,height=9e6,projection='cyl',
lat_1=45.,lat_2=55,lat_0=49.5,lon_0=8.7)
setup_map(m)
m.drawgreatcircle(-10,45,60,45, color='g', lw=3, linestyle='--')
m.drawgreatcircle(0,50,0,0, color='b', lw=3, linestyle='--')
m.plot(np.linspace(-10,60,20), 45*np.ones(20), 'g-', latlon=True, lw=3)
m.plot(np.linspace(0,0,20), np.linspace(50,0,20), 'b-', latlon=True, lw=3)
plt.show()
```

We can see in the output that, even though the dashed curve is actually the shortest distance between two points on the Earth's surface, it's not the shortest distance between two points in the preceding map projection. This is because the cylindrical projection is not a conformal map, but will have great circles appearing as straight lines.

How to draw a day/night terminator

We will make a basemap and apply to it a terminator called `date-time`. The terminator is a division on the Earth's surface between day and night. Use the `nightshade` method that basemap provides and call `utcnow`, as shown here:

```
# Terminator 2: Judgement Datetime (nightshade)
from datetime import datetime
m = Basemap()
setup_map(m)
m.nightshade(datetime.utcnow())
plt.show()
```

We see that it is daytime in Europe and night time in Asia or Australia, and, hence, we can see the curve of the Earth's surface.

To use a different projection, we will use `projection= 'ortho', lan_0=0, lon_0=0`, as shown in the following code:

```
# Terminator 2: Judgement Datetime (nightshade)
from datetime import datetime
m = Basemap(projection='ortho', lat_0=0, lon_0=0)
setup_map(m)
m.nightshade(datetime.utcnow())
plt.show()
```

Hence, we see the terminator now around the edges, with the focus on the latitude at the middle of the day, as shown here:

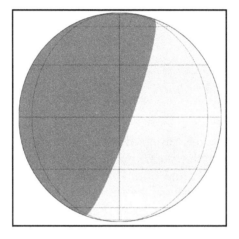

Let's try setting latitude and longitude to 45 degrees:

```
# Terminator 2: Judgement Datetime (nightshade)
from datetime import datetime
m = Basemap(projection='ortho', lat_0=45, lon_0=45)
setup_map(m)
m.nightshade(datetime.utcnow())
plt.show()
```

From the output of the preceding code, we can see the edge of the day/night cycle for the earth:

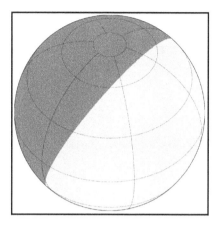

Adding geography

This section describes how to add coastline and water features along with adding political boundaries.

How to add coastline and water features

We will begin by drawing coastlines using the following code:

```
# Just coastlines
m = Basemap(projection='ortho',lon_0=-114, lat_0=51)
m.drawcoastlines()
plt.show()
```

In the previous sections, we have seen that basemap can generate a sort of background image of coastlines of the globe, but we haven't seen how this is done. It is done simply by using the coastlines method in the preceding snippet. Using this gives us the coastlines, as shown in the following output:

In our preceding output, we see that the coastlines are fairly coarse. We can change how coarse the coastlines are by using the `resolution` keyword argument. By default, the resolution is set to the lowest value. We can change the coarseness to low, intermediate, or high. Here, we'll change the coarseness to low, as shown in the following code:

```
# Resolution
m = Basemap(projection='ortho',lon_0=-114, lat_0=51, resolution='l')
m.drawcoastlines()
plt.show()
```

We see that there is an increase in the resolution, as the coastlines become much finer and we actually start to see some features that are basically small lakes that were invisible before. The Hawaiian Islands, which present at the bottom-left of the map can be seen in higher resolution, and you can actually make out the individual islands in Hawaii, whereas previously, only the big island was visible.

So, in order to create a very high resolution plot that includes accurate coastlines and features, and so on, increase the `resolution` keyword argument.

The output for intermediate coarseness and high coarseness takes a while to load, as it involves plotting a higher resolution version of the coastlines.

It is recommended that you change the coarseness to the lowest resolution during the exploratory phase of your data analysis.

How to add political boundaries for countries, states, and provinces

We can also add political boundaries, such as the divisions between nations and states:

1. We get these boundaries by calling the m.drawcountries() function, as shown in the following code:

```
# Countries & states
m = Basemap(projection='ortho',lon_0=-114, lat_0=51)
m.drawcoastlines()
m.drawcountries()
plt.show()
```

The political boundaries can be seen in the following output:

2. The political divisions within countries can also be drawn using the `drawstates( )` function, as shown here:

```
# Countries & states
m = Basemap(projection='ortho',lon_0=-114, lat_0=51)
m.drawcoastlines()
m.drawcountries()
m.drawstates()
plt.show()
```

We get the 50 states of the US, the provinces and territories of Canada, as well as divisions within Mexico and other countries, as shown in the following output:

Hence, basemap actually includes everything you need to draw not only physical boundaries, but political ones as well.

3. We can also add water features (rivers and lakes) using the `basemap` methods, along with the color of the rivers, as shown in the following code:

```
m = Basemap(projection='ortho',lon_0=-114, lat_0=51)
m.drawcoastlines()
m.drawrivers(color='b')
m.fillcontinents(color='none', lake_color='b')
plt.show()
```

We get the following output:

As seen in the preceding output, we can draw lakes, as well as rivers.

Summary

In this chapter, we learned how to plot on 3D axes and how to make various different kinds of plots within those 3D axes. We also studied how to use basemap to generate map projections between the curved surface of the earth and the flat surface of our screens, how to plot onto these map projections and, finally, how to use basemap to add geographical features to the plots that we produced.

In the next chapter, we will learn about interactive plotting, whereby we can make plots that are no longer static images, but actual interactive applications.

5
Interactive Plotting

Until now, we have studied how to plot on 3D axes and how to make various different kinds of plots within those 3D axes. We also studied how to use basemap to generate map projections. Interactive plotting defines a discussion on interactivity wherein Matplotlib plots aren't just static images but dynamic updated figures that can change the way they are displayed based on the changes in real time to actual data in order to build apps using Matplotlib. In this chapter, we will learn about the following topics:

- How to use the `ipywidgets` module with the Jupyter Notebook to make easy, interactive widgets
- How to add callbacks to plots for interactivity
- How to generate GUI neutral widgets for use in different kinds of Matplotlib applications
- How to make movies and animations

Interactive plots in the Jupyter Notebook

This section describes the installation and enabling of the `ipywidgets` module and how to use and customize the different widgets.

How to install and enable the ipywidgets module

Before getting started, we will have to install `ipywidgets`. We will use the `pip install ipywidgets` command to do this. After this has been successfully installed, we need to enable the extension within the Jupyter Notebook. To do that, use the `jupyter nb extension enable - -py widgetsnbextension` command, which will enable the widgets to interact with the Jupyter Notebook.

Begin as usual by importing and setting up the Matplotlib environment, including the `ipywidgets` module, the interactive, fixed, and `interact_manual` methods, as well as `ipywidgets` itself as widgets:

```
import numpy as np
import matplotlib as mpl
import matplotlib.pyplot as plt

from ipywidgets import interact, interactive, fixed, interact_manual
import ipywidgets as widgets
```

To start with, we'll take a look at a simple function that displays a straight line. The `'f'` function of x displays a range of numbers between 0 and 10 with a linear function that has a slope of X. Therefore, f (10), as shown in the following code, gives a linear function with a slope of 10:

```
# Basic interact usage with integer slider
def f(x):
 plt.plot(np.arange(0,10), x*np.arange(0,10))
 plt.ylim(-30,30)
f(10)
```

The following is the output of the preceding code:

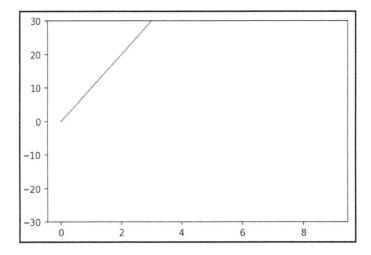

How to use the interact method to make basic widgets

By using the interact method and setting `'x'` to 1 by default we get the following points:

1. The little widget pops up automatically, just above the plot:

```
# Basic interact usage with integer slider
def f(x):
 plt.plot(np.arange(0,10), x*np.arange(0,10))
 plt.ylim(-30,30)
interact(f, x=1)
```

We will get the following output:

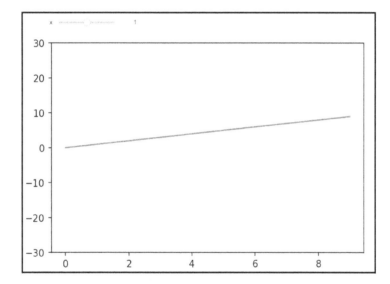

2. Without having to do any extra coding, except for this one very simple function, we actually get an interactive plot. This widget changes the slope of the plot automatically, based on the fact that this argument is an integer. As we change the slider, the line automatically changes, as follows:

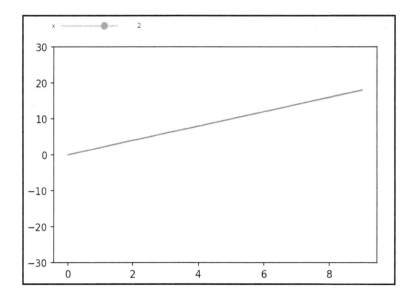

As we change the range of the slider to a bigger or perhaps smaller range, we pass a minimum slope. Let's perform −3 and 3 with a step size of 0.5.

3. From the output, we can see that each click on the slider is 0.5 and going between 3 and −3. The line moves for each click, as shown in the following code:

```
# Range & Step size
def f(x):
  plt.plot(np.arange(0,10), x*np.arange(0,10))
  plt.ylim(-30,30)
interact(f, x=(-3,3,0.5))
```

The following output shows the output for 3.0:

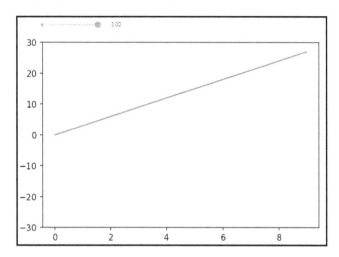

The following output shows the output for -3.0:

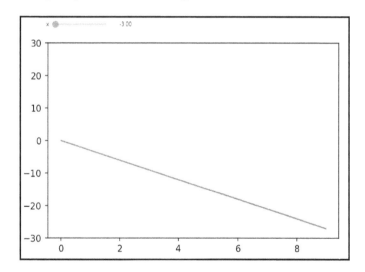

4. Therefore, it is very easy to set up sliders that automatically fill their range. It will choose to use a slider based on the type of the argument:

```
# Automatically choose appropriate widget
rands = np.random.rand(100)
def f(x):
    if x:
        plt.plot(rands, 'b')
```

```
        else:
            plt.plot(rands, 'r')
    interact(f, x=True)
```

While choosing a different function by taking interact (f, x=True), we can see
that it gives a checkbox, as shown in the following output:

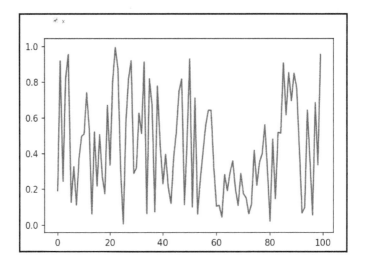

5. When we uncheck this box, we can see that it switches its color, since it's caught
   automatically clearing the output:

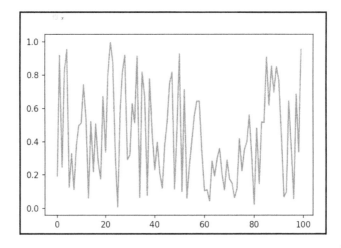

6. The `interact` method can also be passed as a decorator. If, for example, we insert `interact` and pass a string such as `Title of plot`, it gives a textbox, along with the string:

```
# interact as a decorator
@interact(x='Title of plot')
def f(x):
    plt.title(x)
```

The preceding code produces the following output:

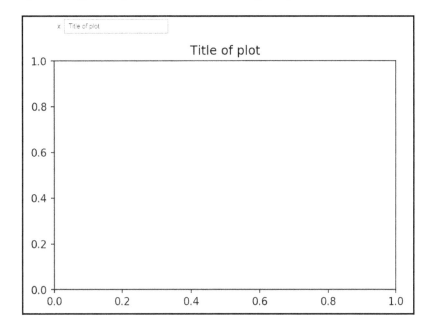

7. The contents of the string can also be changed, and we can see that it automatically feeds into the plot, as shown in the following output:

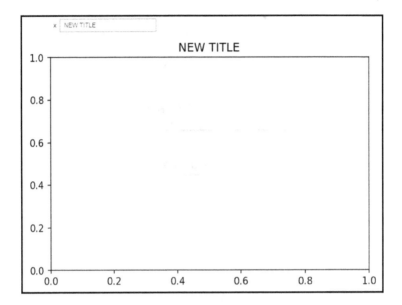

8. We can also choose multiple widgets with the interact method. So, if we have a function that is multivalued, such as a =1, b=3, we automatically get a pair of widgets:

```
# Multiple widgets
def f(a,b):
    plt.plot(np.arange(0,10), a*np.power(np.arange(0,10), b))
    plt.title("Power Law: $x=ay^b$")
interact(f, a=1, b=3)
```

The preceding code will give the following slider just over the plot:

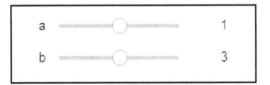

By changing the index of the power law, we get the following output:

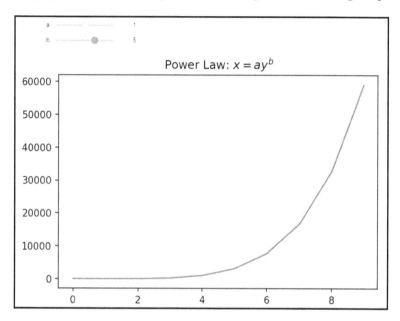

9. Also, by changing the slope of the power law, we get the following output:

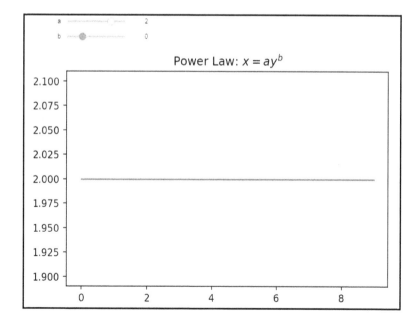

10. The values can also be fixed. Let's say we have two argument functions, such as `a=1` and `b=fixed (2)`, as shown in the following code:

```
# Fixed value
def f(a,b):
    plt.plot(np.arange(0,10), a*np.power(np.arange(0,10), b))
    plt.title("Power Law: $x=ay^b$")
interact(f, a=1, b=fixed(2))
```

By using these argument functions, we get the following output:

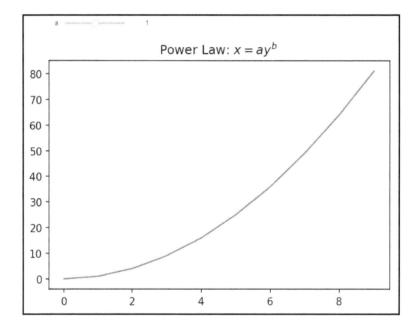

The fixed method that we imported from `ipywidgets` is a method that allows you to automatically set the value of one of these arguments. We could also use an anonymous function, such as `lambda`, but the `ipywidgets` module provides an automatic way to do this without the need to use `lambda` functions.

How to view the different kinds of widgets that ipywidgets provides

We also use the drop-downs that `ipywidgets` provides. To start, let's insert `interact (f, colour=colours)`, as follows:

```
# Dropdowns
def f(colour):
    plt.plot(np.arange(0,10), np.power(np.arange(0,10), 5), c=colour)
    plt.title("Power Law: $x=ay^b$")
colours=['red', 'green', 'blue']
interact(f, colour=colours)
```

A drop-down menu can be seen in the following output. When we select one of the colors from the drop-down, there is a switch between the color of the plot, which means that it's passing that argument to the C argument of the plot, as shown in the following output:

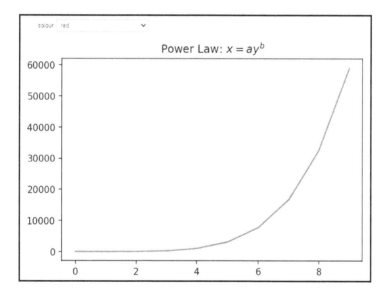

How to customize widgets

In the case where we want a drop-down that does not necessarily pass a string, a dictionary can be passed, as shown in the following code:

```
# Dropdowns with dicts
def f(b):
    plt.plot(np.arange(0,10), np.power(np.arange(0,10), b))
    plt.title("Power Law: $x=ay^b$")
powers = {'one':1, 'two':2, 'three':3}
interact(f, b=powers)
```

In the following output, we have a dictionary with strings for keys. Here, we are passing an integer to the index of the power law.

For power one, we get the following output:

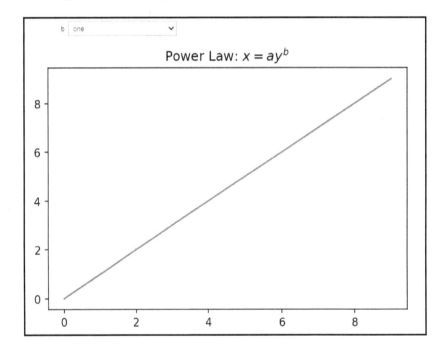

For power `three`, we get the following output:

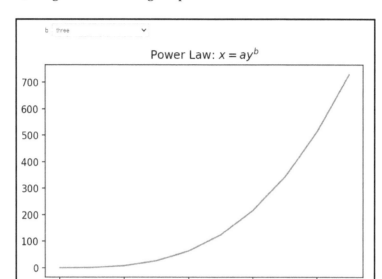

Hence, `ipywidgets` provides a simple way of going from zero to interactivity in no time. There really isn't an easier way to add interactivity to your Matplotlib plots than by using `ipywidgets`.

Event handling with plot callbacks

This section describes how to add interactivity by capturing mouse events along with capturing keyboard clicks.

How to add interactivity by capturing mouse events

Initially, you must import everything that we normally use and use the interactive Notebook backend. Now, the user is not familiar with asynchronous programming with the callback function. This takes in an event, which is then called when that event occurs. The important information of that event is passed as an argument to that function.

We will begin by defining a function called `draw_circle (event)`. These are the events that are passed by Matplotlib callbacks, and they include information about the event. So, in the case of a mouse click, it would be where on the plot the click has occurred.

Call the `plt.plot` function with the x data and the y data of that event, along with a circle. Note that we are calling the `canvas.draw` method on the figure. Here, the `canvas` object that belongs to each figure is essentially the screen object. The `canvas` object actually captures these events and is essentially the lowest-level interface for a figure. Next, add a callback to this canvas using the `mpl_connect` method, along with `button_press_event`:

```
# Mouse click events with button_press_event
plt.plot(np.random.normal(size=100))
def draw_circle(event):
    # Draw a circle
    plt.plot(event.xdata, event.ydata, 'bo')
    # After the figure is updated, re-draw the canvas
    plt.gcf().canvas.draw()
# Add a listener for mouse button press
cid = plt.gcf().canvas.mpl_connect('button_press_event', draw_circle)
```

The output of the preceding code is as follows:

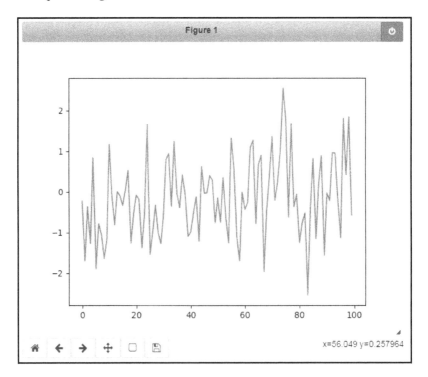

There are a lot of different events that we can add callbacks for. If you're interested in learning more, you can take a look at the Matplotlib documentation: `https://matplotlib.org/contents.html`.

We can see that every time we click on this plot, a small circle is drawn, as shown in the following output:

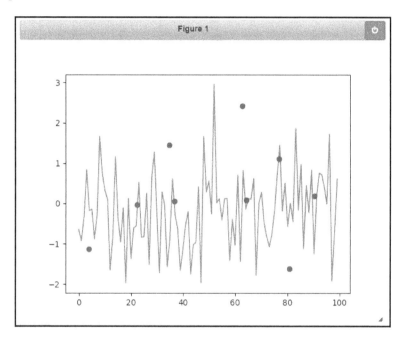

How to capture keyboard clicks

Next, we must capture the return value by inserting `plt.gcf ( )` `.canvas.mpl_disconnect (cid)` to remove the event handler. Therefore, by adding this function, we can click to draw a circle.

However, subsequent clicks will not perform anything as the event handler has been removed:

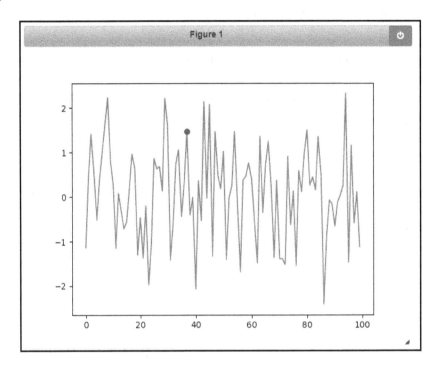

As we can see, the mouse isn't the only thing that can capture events. We can also capture events for key presses. By using the `canvas.mpl_connect` command and passing the first argument as `key_press _event` (the first argument is a string describing which event to capture and the second argument is the callback function), we generate a new plot, as shown in the following code:

```
# Keyboard events with key_press_event
plt.clf()
plt.plot(np.random.normal(size=100))
def redraw(event):
    if event.key == 'r':
        plt.cla()
        plt.plot(np.random.normal(size=100))
        plt.gcf().canvas.draw()
# Add a listener for key presses.
cid = plt.gcf().canvas.mpl_connect('key_press_event', redraw)
```

From the preceding code we will get the following output:

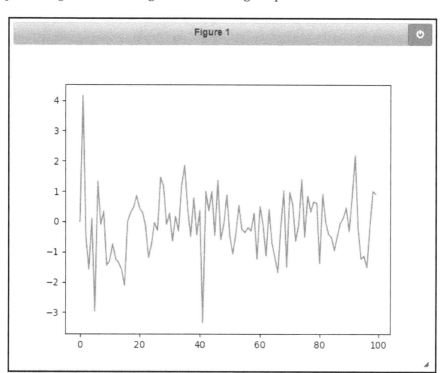

From the preceding output, we can see that if the event.key that is inserted is the r key, it clears the previous image and draws a new, random Markov process.

How to use the picker to manipulate plots

To manipulate the data, we need to add an extra keyword argument called **picker** to our plot, as well as a new function called **gravity** as shown in the following points:

1. What this does is calculate the gravitational force between the particle points within the plot:

```
# Using pick_event & picker to move points
plt.plot(np.random.rand(100), np.random.rand(100), 'ko', picker=5)
def gravity(event):
    thispoint = event.artist
    ind = event.ind[0]
    xpos = thispoint.get_xdata()
```

```
    ypos = thispoint.get_ydata()
    # Calculate the distance to other particles, update their
positions         with a r^-2 law
     rpos = np.linalg.norm([xpos-xpos[ind],ypos-ypos[ind]], axis=0)
    thispoint.set_xdata(xpos - 1e-3*(xpos - xpos[ind])/(1e-
                      9+rpos*rpos))
    thispoint.set_ydata(ypos - 1e-3*(ypos - ypos[ind])/(1e
                      9+rpos*rpos))
    plt.gcf().canvas.draw()

cid = plt.gcf().canvas.mpl_connect('pick_event', gravity)
```

When we run the preceding code, we get the following output:

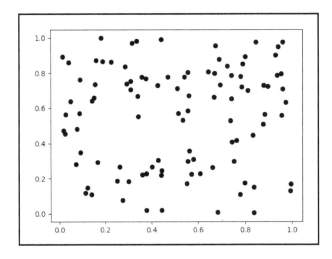

2. We can also change the position of the particles and change their colors as well, as shown in the following code:

```
# Changing colors with pick_event
plt.scatter(np.random.rand(100), np.random.rand(100),
            c=np.random.rand(100), s=80, picker=5,
edgecolor='none')
def color(event):
    # Get the artist object that has been picked
    thispoint = event.artist
    # Get the element (point in this case) that has been picked
    ind = event.ind
    # Get the old face colors
    newcolor = thispoint.get_facecolors()
    # Zero out and re-set the colors
    newcolor[ind] = [0.5,0.5,0.5,1]
```

```
thispoint.set_facecolors(newcolor)
plt.gcf().canvas.draw()
plt.gcf().canvas.mpl_connect('pick_event', color)
```

3. By using this code, we get a scatterplot with randomized colors:

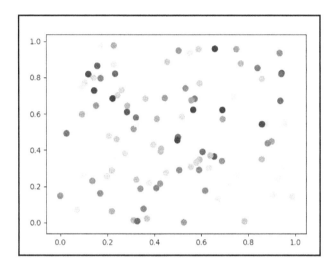

4. When we select any elements, the color changes to gray, as follows:

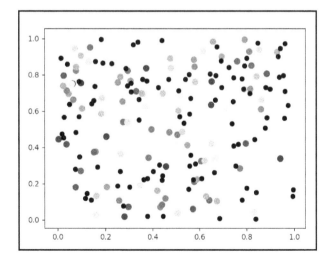

Therefore, we can manipulate any of the standard artist objects and attributes.

To manipulate plot objects, the elements of lines, points, and so on, you can use the pick event. By using the pick event, you can change anything that you can change manually, such as size, hatches, fill, edge colors, and even text.

GUI neutral widgets

This section describes a selection of the different kinds of widgets along with how to add interactivity to these widgets using callbacks.

How to add the basic GUI neutral widgets

We will begin by taking a look at cursor. The cursor will generate a widget that places little *x* axis and *y* axis cursors over the top of the axis. The first argument to any widget is the axis that we want to attach it to. In this case, we want to attach it to the current axis. By doing this, by default, it should look unchanged.

1. However, as we hover over the plot, we get the XY cursor, as shown in the following output after the code:

   ```
   # Basic cursor
   nums = np.arange(0,10,0.1)
   plt.plot(nums, np.sin(nums))
   Cursor(plt.gca())
   ```

   Following is the output of the preceding code:

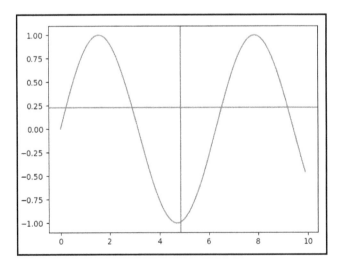

2. As we change the attributes, for example when we change the line width to any other line property (which also changes the color):

```
# Basic cursor
nums = np.arange(0,10,0.1)
plt.plot(nums, np.sin(nums))
Cursor(plt.gca(), linewidth=5, color='r')
```

We will get the following output:

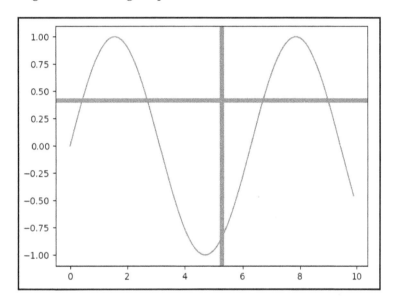

The GUI neutral widgets in Matplotlib are actually modifications to the figure object so that they don't apply widgets to other parts of the code like `ipywidgets` did, where it was using the Jupyter Notebook CEL outputs. Anything that can render a figure can render these GUI neutral widgets, as long as the backend is interactive.

A selection of the different kinds of widgets that are available in Matplotlib

The different selections in Matplotlib are as follows:

1. Generate two axes objects, one that is going to contain a curve and another that is long and thin beneath it, as follows:

```
# Slider
ax1 = plt.axes([0.25, 0.2, 0.65, 0.7])
curve, = ax1.plot(nums, np.sin(nums))
ax1.set_ylim(-10,10)
ax2 = plt.axes([0.25, 0.1, 0.65, 0.03])
def redraw(value):
    curve.set_ydata(value*np.sin(nums))
    plt.gcf().canvas.draw()
amp.on_changed(redraw)
```

We will get the following output:

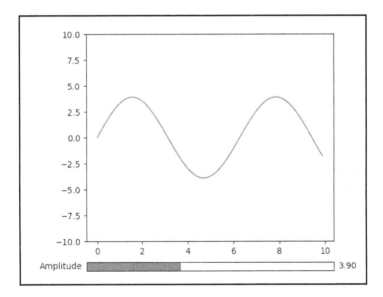

2. Using the long and thin axis underneath, generate a slider, give it ax2 (the long thin one), and call it amplitude. The sliders also have a range; give it a range between 0 and 10, as shown in the following code:

```
# Slider
ax1 = plt.axes([0.25, 0.2, 0.65, 0.7])
curve, = ax1.plot(nums, np.sin(nums))
ax1.set_ylim(-10,10)
ax2 = plt.axes([0.25, 0.1, 0.65, 0.03])
amp = Slider(ax2, 'Amplitude', 0.1, 10, valinit=2)
def redraw(value):
    curve.set_ydata(value*np.sin(nums))
    plt.gcf().canvas.draw()
# amp.on_changed(redraw)
```

When we run the preceding code, we get a little slider widget below the plot. Now, when we click on the slider, it actually changes the value of that slider and the values displayed, as follows:

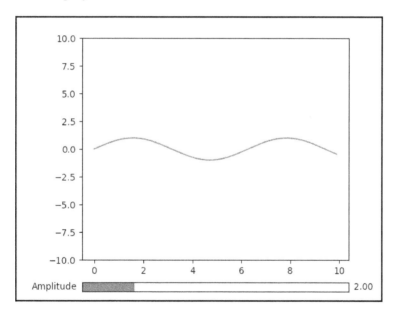

Most of the widgets have methods so that we can apply callbacks on them. In this case, we have the unchanged method for our slider, and we can pass a function that will change the value of this curve.

3. We can generate another set of axes where we have a tiny little box in the corner. By adding a radio button object to that little box with a list as its second argument, `colors`, we can actually fill in a nice little radio button:

```
# Radio Buttons
ax1 = plt.axes([0.05, 0.1, 0.65, 0.8])
curve, = ax1.plot(nums, np.sin(nums))
ax2 = plt.axes([0.75, 0.1, 0.15, 0.3])
colors = ('cyan', 'blue', 'black')
def setcolor(color):
    curve.set_color(color)
    plt.gcf().canvas.draw()
# color.on_clicked(setcolor)
```

The radio button can also be clicked, as shown in the following output:

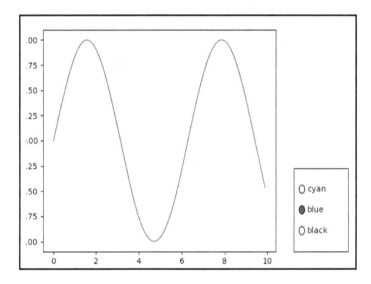

How to add interactivity to these widgets using callbacks

Just like with the slider, we can add a callback in the code that will change the color of our output. By doing this, we can switch between cyan, blue, and black:

```
# Radio Buttons
ax1 = plt.axes([0.05, 0.1, 0.65, 0.8])
curve, = ax1.plot(nums, np.sin(nums))
ax2 = plt.axes([0.75, 0.1, 0.15, 0.3])
```

```
colors = ('cyan', 'blue', 'black')
color = RadioButtons(ax2, colors)
def setcolor(color):
    curve.set_color(color)
    plt.gcf().canvas.draw()
# color.on_clicked(setcolor)
```

We will get the following code:

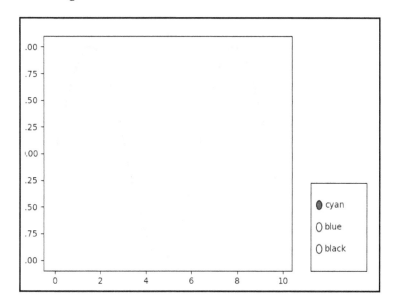

Now, we want to use a selector to select the points in the plot. By doing this, we can generate the selector and add a callback for it. Let's take a look at this callback in passing—you might think from the fact that this is called a rectangle selector that arguments to the callback would be a selection of points—perhaps a line segment—but actually all that gets passed are two events, E1 and E2. The first event is where you click; the second event is where you release the mouse so that these two events cover the two corners of the rectangle that gets drawn:

```
# Using widgets with callbacks
ax1 = plt.subplot(111)
xpts = np.random.rand(100)
ypts = np.random.rand(100)
s = 10*np.ones(100)
points = ax1.scatter(xpts, ypts, s=s, c='b')
ax1.set_xlim(0,1)
ax1.set_ylim(0,1)
def changepoints(e1, e2):
```

```
    x0, x1 = sorted([e1.xdata, e2.xdata])
    y0, y1 = sorted([e1.ydata, e2.ydata])
    sizes = points.get_sizes()
    sizes[np.where((xpts > x0) & (xpts < x1) & (ypts > y0) & (ypts <
            y1))] = 50
    points.set_sizes(sizes)
    plt.gcf().canvas.draw()
rect = RectangleSelector(ax1, onselect=changepoints)
```

To actually select these points, we need to draw a rectangle in this plot and then select where the values of the *x* and *y* positions fall within that rectangle:

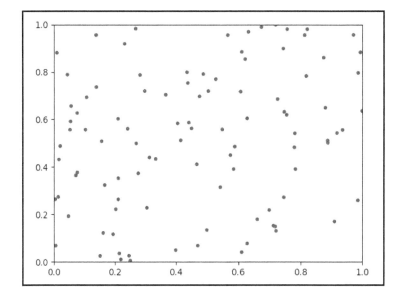

The callback takes the points that have been grabbed within the rectangle selector and increases their size.

This is why here, we can see that the selection is based on the edges of the points that have their X and Y positions within that rectangle. We have also set their sizes using the `set_sizes` method on the return value of that scatterplot by using the `canvas.draw( )` method.

Now, we have seen the workings of the GUI network inside the Jupyter Notebook. We can also do the same outside of the Jupyter Notebook.

Making movies

This section describes how to generate animations to make plots along with customizing the animation frame rate, speed, and repetitions.

How to generate animations to make plots that update themselves

Let's begin by importing the necessary functions and use the Matplotlib Notebook interactive backend. We will also import the FuncAnimation method from Matplotlib.animation.

Start by making the standard basic sine plot. We have also added a function that changes the Y data by moving it over to the first argument. We will now use the func.animation method. As we call the func.animation method with the figure and our update method as the two arguments, we get a nice animation of the sine wave:

```
# Basic FuncAnimation
nums = np.arange(0,10,0.1)
sin, = plt.plot(nums, np.sin(nums))
def update(i):
    sin.set_ydata(np.sin(nums+i))
FuncAnimation(plt.gcf(), update)
```

Following is the output of the preceding code:

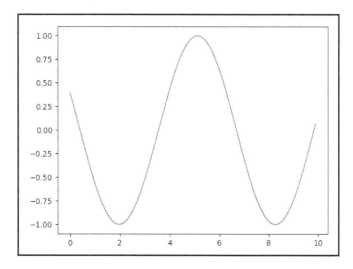

If we set the title to the current value of that argument (`plt.title (i)`), we will see that it will iterate through some integers. By default, `func.animation` will pass subsequent integers to the argument, and so we will see the title updating itself sequentially in integer values. To specify our own values for the animation—let's say we don't want to use integers but drive the sine curve with values between 0 and 2 pi—we can pass the `frames=frames` argument:

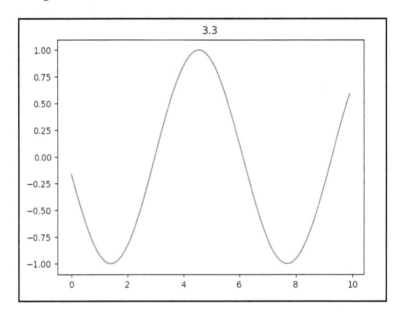

Here, we can see that the sine wave is actually iterating through based on the values from this frames array. When we update the title, we can see that it's actually updating in values, in steps of 0.1, which are the steps of the NumPy array. We can also specify what the interval of the frames is. By default, the interval is set to 200, and the units for that is milliseconds. To update the animation so that it's twice as fast, we can switch it to 100 milliseconds, 50 milliseconds, or all the way down to 10 milliseconds. By doing this, we will see the output updating quite quickly.

 Keep in mind that when we get to very high frame rates, the backend may have difficulty rendering this.

How to customize the animation frame rate, speed, and repetitions

To disable the ability of the animation, set repeat to `False`, as shown in the following code:

```
# Repeat, pause after final frame
nums = np.arange(0,10,0.1)
sin, = plt.plot(nums, np.sin(nums))
frames=np.arange(0,2*np.pi,0.1)
def update(i):
    sin.set_ydata(np.sin(nums+i))
FuncAnimation(plt.gcf(), update, frames=frames, interval=50,
              repeat_delay=2e3)
```

By setting repeat to `False`, we get to loop through the frames array. Then, the animation will halt:

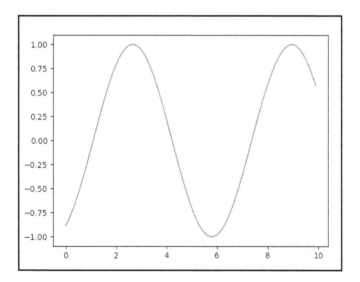

To pause the repetition of the animation, use the `repeat_delay` argument. By using this argument (`repeat_delay=2e3`), we can see that it will rotate through the animation, pause for two seconds, and repeat again.

This is a nice way of stopping the animation to let the viewer know that you're going back to the beginning to repeat the animation:

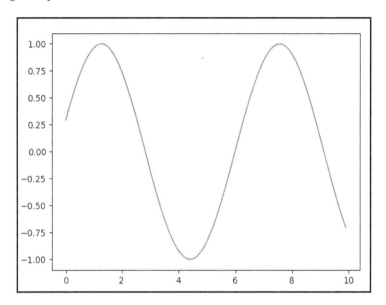

How to save animations as mp4 videos and animated GIFs

Finally, to write these animations instead of having them displayed in the Jupyter Notebook, we need to produce a video or an animated GIF that we can put into a PowerPoint presentation or on a website. To do this, we simply take the return value of the animation and use the `save` method. Hence, by using `anim.save`, we can produce `sine.mp4`, which will take some time to render:

```
# Saving the animation as a mp4 video
nums = np.arange(0,10,0.1)
sin, = plt.plot(nums, np.sin(nums))
frames=np.arange(0,2*np.pi,0.1)
def update(i):
    sin.set_ydata(np.sin(nums+i))
anim = FuncAnimation(plt.gcf(), update, frames=frames, interval=50)
anim.save('sine.mp4')
```

Use the VLC player to play the video that we have produced (`!vlc sine.mp4`). By using VLC on `sine.mp4`, we get an mp4 video, which automatically produces the requisite output.

To produce an animated `.gif`, we need to pass in the `writer` argument to specify what will write this out. We will use an argument called `ImageMagick`, which is a commonly used toolkit on most systems. By running `!eog sine.gif`, we get an animated `.gif`.

By using these animation toolkits that Matplotlib provides, it is actually quite easy to produce movies and animations in Matplotlib. A couple of years ago, that wasn't the case, but this toolkit has matured quite significantly in the last few years.

Summary

In this chapter, we have learned about Jupyter Notebook and `ipywidgets`. We also studied how to add interactivity with callbacks in Matplotlib for mouse click and keyboard events.

We learned how to add GUI neutral widgets that work both in the Jupyter Notebook and with any other kind of interactive backend, which is really useful for building applications with Matplotlib. Finally, we learned that animations and movies are very easy to do with simple updater functions that can write out to video files and animated GIFs.

Other Books You May Enjoy

If you enjoyed this book, you may be interested in these other books by Packt:

Matplotlib 3.0 Cookbook
Srinivasa Rao Poladi

ISBN: 9781789135718

- Develop simple to advanced data visualizations in Matplotlib
- Use the pyplot API to quickly develop and deploy different plots
- Use object-oriented APIs for maximum flexibility with the customization of figures
- Develop interactive plots with animation and widgets
- Use maps for geographical plotting
- Enrich your visualizations using embedded texts and mathematical expressions
- Embed Matplotlib plots into other GUIs used for developing applications
- Use toolkits such as axisartist, axes_grid1, and cartopy to extend the base functionality of Matplotlib

Matplotlib for Python Developers - Second Edition
Aldrin Yim, Claire Chung, Allen Yu

ISBN: 9781788625173

- Create 2D and 3D static plots such as bar charts, heat maps, and scatter plots
- Get acquainted with GTK+3, Qt5, and wxWidgets to understand the UI backend of Matplotlib
- Develop advanced static plots with third-party packages such as Pandas, GeoPandas, and Seaborn
- Create interactive plots with real-time updates
- Develop web-based, Matplotlib-powered graph visualizations with third-party packages such as Django
- Write data visualization code that is readily expandable on the cloud platform

Leave a review - let other readers know what you think

Please share your thoughts on this book with others by leaving a review on the site that you bought it from. If you purchased the book from Amazon, please leave us an honest review on this book's Amazon page. This is vital so that other potential readers can see and use your unbiased opinion to make purchasing decisions, we can understand what our customers think about our products, and our authors can see your feedback on the title that they have worked with Packt to create. It will only take a few minutes of your time, but is valuable to other potential customers, our authors, and Packt. Thank you!

Index